MINDFUL RELATIONSHIP HABITS

HOW TO IMPROVE COMMUNICATION IN YOUR MARRIAGE OR RELATIONSHIP AND ENHANCE EMOTIONAL INTIMACY IN JUST 25 MINUTES A DAY

SOPHIE IRVINE

© **Copyright 2019 - All rights reserved.**

The content contained within this book may not be reproduced, duplicated or transmitted without direct written permission from the author or the publisher.

Under no circumstances will any blame or legal responsibility be held against the publisher, or author, for any damages, reparation, or monetary loss due to the information contained within this book. Either directly or indirectly.

Legal Notice:

This book is copyright protected. This book is only for personal use. You cannot amend, distribute, sell, use, quote or paraphrase any part, or the content within this book, without the consent of the author or publisher.

Disclaimer Notice:

Please note the information contained within this document is for educational and entertainment purposes only. All effort has been executed to present accurate, up to date, and reliable, complete information. No warranties of any kind are declared or implied. Readers acknowledge that the author is not engaging in the rendering of legal, financial, medical or professional advice. The content within this book has been derived from various sources. Please consult a licensed professional before attempting any techniques outlined in this book.

By reading this document, the reader agrees that under no circumstances is the author responsible for any losses, direct or indirect, which are incurred as a result of the use of information contained within this document, including, but not limited to, — errors, omissions, or inaccuracies.

CONTENTS

Introduction	5
Chapter 1: My Relationship is Falling Apart! How Do I Fix It?	11
Chapter 2: Mindfulness — Is It Really That Powerful?	18
Chapter 3: The Top Mindful Relationship Habits to Utilize!	23
Chapter 4: Using Emotional Intelligence to Fix Your Relationship!	44
Chapter 5: Emotional Intelligence Relationship Practices	49
Chapter 6: Establishing Emotional Intimacy	71
Chapter 7: Spicing Up Your Sex Life With Sexual Intelligence	96
Bonus Chapter: Improve your Communication Using Emotional Management	120
Conclusion	141
Resources	143

INTRODUCTION

Let's face it, building the perfect relationship is never easy.

Sometimes, we think everything is good, but there is a feeling of boredom, a feeling that it's not fresh and fun anymore.

This is a problem a lot of couples in our society face.

Oftentimes, we feel like our relationship is tanking, and we're just struggling to create the perfect life with our partner. This worry leads to us feeling scared to expand and grow as a couple, and for couples, they may feel like they're just going to continue in this way.

Do you sometimes feel like the spark has gone? Like you're just bored with your relationship? Do you feel like you're slowly not understanding your partner as much, or you're distancing yourself?

This is a big problem for lots of people. They want to avoid the conflicts, but that leads to them not talking to their partner about what's going on.

The other issue is that couples take their lives for granted many times. They struggle to feel like they're doing the right thing, and for many couples, they're just floundering on by.

What's the solution to this?

Well, read on to find out!

The Solution: Becoming Mindful!

This might seem a bit vague, but mindfulness is the solution to a relationship that's tanking, a relationship that feels stale and boring.

Why is that? Well when's the last time you thought about what you were doing, or maybe noticed and were thankful for your partner? If you can't figure out the answer to that, then you need mindfulness.

Mindful relationship habits will help you figure out the best choices for you, and your partner. You'll have practical options that you can try, and different exercises that will help you become more mindful and improve your relationship with your partner.

Whether you struggle with physical intimacy, having a deeper love and connection, or even issues with trust, becoming mindful of your partner is one of the best ways to rectify this problem. Lots of people don't realize how much of an impact this can have on you, but mindfulness is the solution, and the best means to change your life.

Why is that? Well, becoming more knowledgeable of what's going on will help you connect with your partner, so if there is a problem, you guys talk it out instead of just ignoring the elephant in the room. It will change you, and it will help bring that spark right back into the relationship.

Why You NEED to Read This Book

Emotional intimacy is something we all can do better. You need to become more aware of what your partner is going through. After all, if you're not aware, can you help them.

How many times have you seen your partner look upset, but never checked on them, or didn't even realize they were going through issues themselves? How many times have you felt the spark in the bedroom start to die away? You don't want to lose the person that you love, but something needs to give. You have to do something about this.

And that's why you need this book!

This book is the best way to help you figure out how to become more connected with your partner, to reach a deeper, more thoughtful understanding of what is going on in their life. Mindfulness is one of the keys to success, and one of the keys to wellness for not just yourself, but your partner, and you need to understand how much this matters.

This book will teach you, in just 25 minutes a day, how to

build emotional intelligence, regulate anger, become mindful of what you say to your partner, and also build a better relationship.

Building relationships does take time, of course, but if you put the time in, you'll get the results. I know that I did. I had a failing relationship myself. It felt like I was floundering around, unsure of the solutions to my issues, but once I started using these practices, for less than half an hour a day, I was able to build a happier, more fruitful relationship with the person I loved. It changed my life, and it can sure change your life too.

So yes, you'll want to continue reading. By the end of this book, you'll understand the power of mindfulness, and how to communicate better in your relationship. I know it can be hard, and I know repairing a relationship that might've hit a few hurdles isn't always easy, but with the right mindset, and the right understanding, you'll be much happier as well, and you'll be able to, with the right techniques, create a better life for everyone.

I want you to succeed, I want you to do better, I started using mindfulness myself in my relationship, and it changed my life. I can help you create that change in your own life as well, you just need to understand what needs to be done, and understand the importance of your own personal life, and the life of your partner. Growing as a couple is something you do together, and you should make sure that you have a strong foundation to move forward. I can provide that foundation in this book, and as you continue reading, you'll learn the power of mindfulness, and growth with these practical activities that anyone can do!

So, what are you waiting for? It's time for you to figure out how you can become a better, stronger person and make your relationship more awesome than ever before with these helpful tips!

CHAPTER 1: MY RELATIONSHIP IS FALLING APART! HOW DO I FIX IT?

Are you already on a sinking ship? This might be the problem you're facing now, and I understand it can be stressful. But there are reasons as to why relationships fall apart, and here, we'll discuss why that happens, and how you can take it upon yourself to fix it.

The Key Reasons Why You're Struggling to Stay Together

So why are you struggling to stay together? Well, surprise, surprise, there are a few culprits behind it. Here, we'll talk about the key reasons why couples break up, and how you can prevent this.

Communication Errors

Communication is the way to solve all the problems in life, but a lack thereof is the best way to create problems. Do you ever have an argument and think about where the communication went wrong?

Some people either don't listen to their partner, don't let their partner speak and instead talk on and on about what they're upset about, or even worse, they don't bother to check on their partner. Have you seen those relationships that are basically just two people living together with nothing deeper? It's a sad situation, but often communication is the solution to your problems.

Also, here's the reality of it: almost all problems are a result of not communicating or miscommunication. Are your needs not being met? Communicate that! Even not being loyal comes down to communicating. Some partners may have something they're missing, and while obviously there is no excuse for cheating whatsoever especially in this day and age, you need to communicate the problems in life. The worst thing for you to do is go on without talking. If nothing else, learn to develop that, which is one of the key elements of this book.

Not Enough Time and Effort

Okay, every time someone says there isn't enough time, nine times out of ten they're full of it. There is always time, always ways to make an effort for you to stay together, and ways to make it all work. You need to pay attention to this. Spend time with one another, and if you're not creating enough time for them, you're setting yourself up for breakup, and from there, it'll be nothing but trouble.

This also comes down to communicating. If you don't put the time aside to talk, you're going to fail.

Trust (or Lack Thereof)

Again, this also does boil down to communication. There are those partners who notice something a bit strange, but don't ask their partner about it. Perhaps they see their partner spending more time with a friend than they used to, or their husband going out with the boys more. If you feel like there's something amiss, do talk things over in a reliable manner. Being open and honest with your partner leaves no room for jealousy and suspicion.

Sometimes, people break up because they THINK their partner is cheating or doing something wrong, and they end up getting paranoid. But, if you just talked things out, wouldn't that fix the whole mess? It's so simple, but lots of people fail to do this for that reason alone.

Not Willing to Compromise

This is something partners don't realize is going to cause trouble over time. A compromise needs to happen in every relationship. You need to be ready and willing to compromise at any point in your relationship to make things work. Here's the truth of it: often, we never fully compromise. Our mindset is usually "my way or the highway" and at the bottom of it all is usually stubbornness.

This also comes down to your partner too. Do you find yourself nagging about your partner and being kind of a shit about the little things? Well, you have to realize that nobody is perfect, and if you're upset about something in the past, you're going to continue to hold onto that upset for a while. You need to start learning to let these go.

This also comes down to learning to appreciate your partner. If you can't see the good in them, and you feel like you're just bothered by them, you're going to feel the passion completely dissipate. This happens. This is where the "nagging wife" trope comes about, and it just makes trouble for everyone. Though dubbed the "nagging wife", it doesn't mean it only applies to women.

Even if it's a little bit of a hard thing to do, you've got to learn to compromise.

While yes, people do change, it's important to understand that usually, these are the causes of problems in the relationship. If you start to notice the spark beginning to die or fade with time, then it may be time to look for the culprit.

How to Build and Keep a Relationship Fresh to Avoid Heartbreak

So how do you build it? Well for starters, this book will provide a lot of practices, and practical applications to help you get the most that you can out of your relationship.

But it does come down to a few key things. For starters, please start communicating. If nothing else, describe your problems, even just the little nuances of life. Don't be afraid to do that, cause chances are, that's part of the reason you're suffering in the first place.

Next, spend time with one another. Build this intimacy up again. Most people don't even realize they're struggling with intimacy with their partner until it's too late, when their partner says that they're unhappy. Intimacy is usually just fully linked to sex, but it also involves emotional closeness and non-sexual physical intimacy. When was the last time you really hugged your partner, when you felt that love from them, when you were in the moment?

You also need to make time to implement these. I get it, we're all busy, that's a fact of life. But here's the truth of it: we're not so busy that we can't spend time with the person that we love, that in some cases we said "I do" to. I understand that kids, work, the nagging mother-in-law, and the like can be quite a nightmare to deal with, but if you're struggling, you need to spend time with the other person. You need to learn how to put your foot down and tell your partner that you do care, that you love them, and you want to make things better for them.

This is how you do it. You need to sit down, make time, and really make it work.

In this book, we'll also be pushing mindfulness too, many times, we don't even realize how unmindful we are of what's going on, but if you ever feel like your relationship is a bit dull, or you're just going through the motions, then you need to start becoming mindful. You'd be amazed at the difference, and you'll be able to change this.

Finally, you need to learn how to handle upsets, to understand your partner better, and to even manage your own anger as well. We're all human, but if you don't know how to effectively change the outcome of the issue at hand, to handle the upset so everyone is happy, you're both going to be upset, and it's not going to be fun. Do yourself a favor and learn how to do this.

Fortunately, all of these issues can get resolved here, we'll tackle each of these problems, and show to you how you can become the best person you can be, and how you can become the person that will make your partner happy.

You need to start taking this matter into your own hands, to appreciate your partner for who they are, and this book will help you.

Now obviously, change and the like can happen too, and while yes, at the end of the day, people can change that's not the sole reason for this. Instead, it has more to do with how you treat your partner, and how you go about making them happy. Learning this will help you become a better person not just to your partner, but to yourself as well. Don't be afraid to try, because it could change you.

CHAPTER 2: MINDFULNESS — IS IT REALLY THAT POWERFUL?

Mindfulness is essential for relationships. For many, it's the sole means to change the way you see your partner, and in other ways, it lets you look at the reality of the situation, so you can fix it immediately. But what is mindfulness, and how will it save your relationship? Read on to find out.

Just What is Mindfulness

Mindfulness, at the core at least, is being aware of what you're doing, and in the moment.

That's easier said than done.

Do you ever feel like you just robotically go through the motions, whether it be cuddling, kissing, or even taking a shower? That's an example of not being mindful.

Being mindful entails you being aware of just what you're doing, and how you can change the outcome of what's happening.

Being mindful is great for relationships, and it can help you build your connection to newer levels. It allows you to be more aware, and it can have a positive impact on what you're going through.

Being mindful helps with being aware, and you'll pay more attention to your partner, thereby helping you with building a happier and more improved relationship. It can impact your brain as well.

How Does It Help?

How can this help? Well, do you sometimes feel like you're not in the moment when you're talking to your partner? This autopilot is something we all do in life, and sometimes, we don't realize it.

Sometimes, one of the common reasons why people won't listen to you is because their attention isn't on you, but instead on their phone, what they're listening to, or even just spaced out. This is a great way to kind of pull you back into the moment, helping you be more present, and helps you stay more connected.

It also kind of stops those negative emotional reactions that will happen when you're talking about hard subjects with your partner. Sensitive topics can make us reactive, but mindfulness can help with regulating the amygdala, which is that little part of the brain that causes the "fight or flight" mode. We rely on this when there are fights that happen. Mindfulness can reduce the impact of this, and instead of us relying on reactionary measures, and in turn can help with that arguing that happens and also prevents the emotional distances that happen after you have fights. I'm not sure of the meaning! If you notice that you fight a lot, this is something that can impact those fights and reduce them.

There is also the fact that it can help with improving the prefrontal cortex communication as well. If your prefrontal cortex is present in the moment, it will basically tell the amygdala that hey, everything is cool, you don't need to worry, so even when we're upset or start to lose it, we can become mindful of what's happening, stop the arguments, and prevent ourselves from going down that rabbit hole. In turn it can help with regulating the emotions that occur during fights.

So basically, it can help you stop acting irrationally when you've got to talk about issues with your partner.

It also builds self-awareness, since it will help with tackling the anterior cingulate cortex, which helps to regulate your emotions and how you act in issues. Mindfulness helps us observe whenever we're acting in ways we shouldn't be acting, and from there, puts the brakes on that so we can start behaving better, becoming more in-tune with what we're doing. It helps retrain those destructive or manipulative impulses, and it may also help you get things done, especially when you feel like you're going to do something that you might regret.

This is especially helpful whenever you sense those feelings of distrust in your body. Sometimes, when we're not trusting, we tend to act irrationally, even trying to break into our partner's items or try to stalk their online activity. If you believe your partner, you won't do that, and mindfulness can help prevent that from happening.

Finally, it helps build empathy and makes us empathic. Being an empath can be hard to deal with, and you may be one yourself, but if you sometimes feel like you really don't understand your partner, or don't get where they're coming from, mindfulness can help. Mindfulness can help with regulating the areas of the brain that are responsible for compassion, along with empathy, making it better to understand things from our partners perspective, the emotions that we feel, and we sense more compassion from them.

Instead of feeling angry, or wanting to control, we approach the issues with compassion and understanding. This can help turn the negative situation into that of a positive one. It also helps with expressing love, which will build intimacy on many levels. It also helps you approach, rather than avoid the issues at hand, and that's a big part of relationships. It's much better to face the music than it is to avoid it.

So yes, you need to be more mindful. This chapter showed the impact it can have, and other reasons why mindfulness may matter.

CHAPTER 3: THE TOP MINDFUL RELATIONSHIP HABITS TO UTILIZE!

So, what mindfulness relationship habits should you use? Thankfully, there's a lot that you can do, and a lot that can benefit you in different ways. Here are 11 relationship habits that utilize mindfulness, in order to help you get the most out of your relationship.

Practice 1: Your Relationship Vision

This is the first practice you should use. Why is this so important? Well, how many times do you feel like you're going through the motions at hand, and you feel like you're not entirely happy with the outcomes at hand? Your relationship does matter, and the vision that you have for the relationship is just as important as the relationship itself.

So how do you get better with this? The answer is improving the vision you have of the relationship!

Improving the relationship vision will help you understand your partner much better and get a much better result from what you do with them. It will help you stay grounded and allow you to make the right decisions.

So how do you do this? Well, follow the steps below:

1. You should start doing this alone to begin, since it's what you want in your relationship.

2. Get a piece of paper and write down the goal of the relationship. Be as honest and as detailed as you can.

3. From there, write down how you can get that goal, and figure out how to achieve it with *Actionable* ways.

4. From there, write down how your partner contributes to this, and how they contribute to the perfect relationship vision.

5. Write down how you can contribute to this perfect relationship vision, and the best means to do it.

6. At this point, sit down with your partner and tell them your vision of the relationship.

7. From there, tell them what you plan to do, and that they can input what they want to do in order to help with this.

8. Once both of you have agreed on this, keep this vision and goal somewhere where you can see it, such as on the fridge.

9. Every day look at it and become mindful of what you're doing. From there, you can focus your actions on the relationship vision, rather than just floundering around hoping that something will work.

Sometimes, the first thing you need to do is envision what you want out of the relationship. This is the goal the two of you have together, the end-game for everyone. With the right mindset and the right understanding, you'll create the right pathway. This can take a while, especially if you feel your relationship is on the rocks already. But, understanding your vision, and getting a grasp on what you want out of your relationship is so important, that if you don't have that, you're going to struggle with the rest of this.

Set the goal in place, and you'll make changes.

Practice 2: Visualizing Three Great Things About Your Partner

This one is for the naggers out there.

Joking aside, sometimes the reason why we don't feel happy is because we haven't appreciated and been mindful of our partner in a bit.

Not being mindful of your partner is a road to problems. Sometimes, we need to figure out why this is happening, and why we can't be happy. Being able to visualize three great things about your partner will help you learn to appreciate them, and help you understand the troubles you're going through better.

For those who are on a sinking ship but want to patch the problems up, this is a great practice to begin with.

This one is something you do alone, since the goal of this here is to make sure that you're happy about your partner, and you're appreciative of them.

To do this, start with the following:

1. First, sit in a quiet space, with no distractions about, along with a pencil and paper or a notebook.

2. From there, envision your partner. Think about them for a little while.

3. At this point, think about three things that you like about them, and then write them down.

4. If you discover it's effortless to write three things that you like or find great about your partner, then envision three more.

5. If you start to feel the evil or nagging thoughts come in,

ignore those. They are not what you're worried about, and that could engross your attention. Just focus on the good.

6. Continue to focus on the good, and from there, once you've written down a lot of good things about your partner, close your eyes, and focus on those. If you notice intrusive thoughts, start to acknowledge them, but don't get hung up on them.

7. If you start to notice your mind is going to those nagging, negative feelings, acknowledge this and from there continue on.

8. When you have done this for about five minutes, open your eyes. You'll find your mind is much clearer than it was before, while also feeling much happier…

9. Next time there is a stressful situation, think about those good things that your partner has, and the good in them. Focus on that, and actively listen to them, instead of nagging.

This can be difficult if you're the type to point out faults, but remember that this is the person you're with, and if you constantly point out the flaws, you're never going to be happy.

Practice 3: Understanding Relationship Problems

This one is learning to acknowledge that there are relationship problems. Knowing is half the battle, and if you can figure out the problem, and the solution with your partner, this can ultimately help you become better at maintaining a relationship with them.

Now, you can do this alone, or with your partner. Some people like to do this with their partner, since you both are strong enough to understand the problem, and you both are a team. Sometimes tackling this as a team works. Plus, it lets the partner speak up on anything they want to say about the problems at hand.

To begin, do the following:

1. Sit in a room together, with no distractions, and a piece of paper with the goal at hand.

2. Sit there and discuss one of the problems. Speak one at a time, and from there, talk about the issue at hand.

3. Discuss this issue at hand and pose solutions to one another. Both of you need to say something on the solution to this, and from there, you should both be on the same page on what you choose to do about the issue.

4. If there are issues, sit there, and be quiet for a moment, and talk with your partner. Let them speak about the issue that they have with it. At that point, acknowledge and tell your side.

5. From there, you both sit there and work out the problem, including the steps to fix the issue.

6. Continue to do this with all of the problems, and from there, tackle the easiest problem first, and work on them together.

This step is best done together because it's something you both need to work on with one another and get a feeling for. Getting an understanding of what is happening, and any problems that are cropping up within the relationship will help.

And if you notice that you feel naggy or upset about your partner, take what we did beforehand and visualize three good things about them at that moment, and then, you'll find yourself start to relax, and in turn, build a much better foundation to begin with.

Practice 4: Working on Goals and Dreams

This is basically the flip side to practice 3. Yes, you have problems, and understanding those problems is important, but what about the goals and dreams? This isn't just something that you do by yourself either. I would like for you to do this one with your partner if possible. If not, do it by yourself.

The best thing about this is you can be honest about what you want, and if nothing else, communicate this. Getting together and sitting down, talking out the issue and communicating, is super important for couples. That's because people avoid the issue, but being mindful of the goals and the dreams you have is so essential, and here, we'll discuss how to do it.

To begin, you do the following:

1. Either both of you sit together, or you sit alone.

2. Write down all of the goals and dreams that you have that are major goals. These can be large.

3. Understand that these goals take time and write down the process that you need to consider in order to achieve this.

4. From here, if you're working with your partner, tell them about this. Have them acknowledge and understand.

5. Find out what their goals and dreams are. Sit down and work out a plan to get what both of you want to be done together.

6. If you notice your goals and dreams differ on some points, understand that's a factor of life. Everyone has different goals and dreams.

7. With the minor goals, sit there and work out a plan that both of you can do together. Both of you should work together and figure out for yourself how you can do this.

8. If your goals differ, instead of being upset about it, you should both work towards a compromise, and figure out how everyone can be happy.

With goals and dreams, you should understand that there are many different reasons for why these exist, and while your partner may not have the same goals as you, it's very important to understand that building goals together, understanding the other person's dreams, and making it works will help with building a brighter, better future for both of you. Your goals and dreams matter and working together on these is a must.

If you have done this one alone, sit down with your partner and communicate it with them. If you can, have them do the same. This will get both of you on track to success, and to understanding one another much better.

Practice 5: Setting Personal Boundaries

Boundaries in relationships are essential and being mindful of the limits you would like to have is incredibly important.

We do take our boundaries for granted, but everyone needs their space. Even if they don't say it outright, they need it. Boundaries are what keep us individual, and for many, unhappiness in relationships stems from the lack of limits.

You see this many times in people who have been together with their partner for so long that they think that it's okay to take on the personality of their partner. But that's a road that will only make you unhappy, so you need to learn personal boundaries, and understand why they're there.

How do you set them? Well, read below and try this exercise.

1. First, sit down in a space that's quiet and not filled with distractions

2. From here, write down what you're doing in life

3. Write down the boundaries that you can set up

4. Start to implement a process where you put those rules in

5. Work on trying to build these boundaries with yourself, and your partner

Now, boundaries don't always mean you're shooing someone out, you're supposed to have limits in order to stay grounded and happy. How many times have you felt like you're just robotically doing everything your partner does. You need to maintain your individuality in order to be happy and sometimes the reason why you feel stuck in your relationship is because you're not putting boundaries up.

Even if it's just 30 minutes of personal time to yourself, whether that be reading, gaming, or whatever, put it in place. You can have your own interests while still being in a relationship. That's a big thing people forget. You need to do this, or else you're going to go crazy.

Practice 6: Mindfulness Money Management

Ahh, money! It can sometimes be the one issue you have in your relationship. It can also potentially affect the outcome of your relationship too. If you have issues with money, realize you're not alone. Money management is one of the hardest things, but being mindful about your money can change everything.

Becoming mindful of your money, and where it's going will help you keep your priorities straight, and also prevent upsets with your partner. Personally, this is one I recommend doing with your partner, and it doesn't need to be something you do in just one day. It can be a transitioning process but being mindful of where your money is going is essential.

Understanding where it's going can also help you become aware of habits that are harmful to you, and habits that are inevitably very costly. Which, we all tend to have of course.

Our vices are sometimes various actions we don't even recognize, but with the right mindfulness and energies, you can understand this better, and build a better future.

To become more mindful with money, you need to do the following:

1. First, get you and your partner both in on this, and sit down in a space with not too many distractions, but you can access your finances

2. Sit down and write down your average earnings

3. From there take away what you have to spend money on

4. Look at the leftovers, and talk about your habits with one another

5. Decide whether or not those habits are important, and whether you need them. If you don't, you can eliminate them.

6. At this point, look at any vices that you have, and anything that eats your money.

7. Start to become aware of your finances, and from there, make agreements on where you're putting the money

8. If you have a joint bank account, you both need to put the list together. If you're separate, you both need to be aware of your own separate finances

9. Also, look at your goals, and start to plan for those goals. For example, if you want to go on vacation to another country, look at where you can give up things, so you can help feed money into that.

10. From there, become mindful of every transaction, and if you notice that you don't need it, then obviously don't buy it

Obviously, if you're the type who loves to spend money, this is much easier said than done, but with the right attitude, and the right awareness, you'll be able to create a much healthier mindset and be able to focus on your own personal endeavors in a much healthier manner. Mindfulness in money is critical, so don't forget that.

Practice 7: Being Aware of Your Partner's Concerns

Sometimes, your partner may have some issues that you're not particularly aware of. One way for fights to happen, is not being aware of these. Sometimes though, you might know about them, and other times, it may not be the case.

If the latter is more of what's going on, you need to start building awareness of your partner's concerns. Whether you know them or not, you need to sit down with the person you're with and voice these concerns. This is something that can help you with communicating too.

The best way to do this is to have your partner voice them to you, and write them down, and from there, become aware of your partner and what they're worried about so you can make sure you don't press their buttons or upset them.

To do this, begin with the following:

1. Sit down with one another in a quiet place with little to no other elements around to distract you.

2. From there, ask your partner what they're worried about. Have them tell you everything that's going on.

3. You can write it down, or just listen and take notes. Acknowledge and thank them for telling you what's happening.

4. From there, both of you need to start putting together the best means to go about preventing this from happening. For example, if your partner is worried about spending money frivolously, you can work together and figure out a good spending routine to keep it all in mind. If your partner doesn't like it when you interrupt them, you need to become more aware of that.

5. The next step is more of a personal thing. Sit down and think about your partner's concerns. Think about what you can do in order to make sure that you're providing the best and healthiest relationship between both of you. Think about how you can prevent their buttons from being pressed.

6. Finally, meditate on it, and the next time you notice something is wrong, ask your partner. Get them to tell you and show to them that their concerns matter, and you want to help them.

Learning to understand your partner's concerns is essential. If you don't understand what's bothering your partner, then are you going to be happy? The answer is of course not. You're both going to be upset, and it's not going to be fun for anyone. So, make sure that, if there are upsets here, you talk about them, and you both work together to build a better, healthier relationship that works for both of you, so you're not upset with one another. Understanding is the key to success, both in relationships and in life in general.

Practice 8: Deep Listening and Why You Gotta Do It!

How much do you really listen to your partner?

Oftentimes, we feel like the words spoken from most go in one ear, and then out the other. This is a result of the way our minds typically work, and because of this we get ourselves in trouble. Have you ever upset your partner simply because you weren't listening? This happens more than you'd think, but with deep listening, you can start to listen to your partner better, and build more awareness.

Just how do you do it? Well, the process of deep listening is where you're aware of what is going on, without judging it immediately. When you hear someone speak, how many times do you think immediately about what that has to do with you? Probably more than you care to admit. The reality is the reason why you're having trouble is you don't listen to your partner, but being open, fresh, kind, and alert to the issues at hand will help you keep everything better.

It also promotes active listening. We typically practice static listening, but active listening helps you build better practice and instruction, and you should essentially pay attention to what someone is saying, without getting into the habits that you have, such as thinking about what you're going to say or interrupting the person.

Oftentimes, the reason why we struggle with relationships is we don't listen. We're planning what we want to say next, and that's where interruptions come in. Have you ever interrupted your partner without meaning to? There you go, you're not actively listening.

Being mindful of your own listening encourages you to take in what someone is saying, understand the meaning, and give better responses. Plus, it curbs that interruption that you want to make.

To begin, you must do the following:

1. Sit in a quiet place in a stable position, and tall, such as with your legs crossed or in a chair with a supportive back. Be alert, but also relaxed too and close your eyes.

2. From there, listen to any sounds as they occur, even if it's just the sound of nothingness

3. Don't try to analyze, imagine, or do anything with it. But instead, listen.

4. You may start to notice distractions, and as they happen, return these back to the sounds, and listen with awareness.

5. Let the sounds completely come in, and as sounds hit, with emotions, thoughts and memories attached, let them go and then return to the sounds once again.

6. From here, notice as they rise and then fall away, but don't grasp, reject, or do anything there.

7. If you notice no sounds, just understand and listen to the silence.

8. After about 10 minutes, open your eyes, and think about whether or not in the daily life you have positive and negative habits that come with listening, and what you can do to listen without judgement.

9. You can from here, write them down, and work on trying to listen without these habits falling in.

From here, practice this in conversation. Work on sitting without an agenda attached to it, so you can listen to what the other person is saying, and in turn, it will help you build self-control, resulting in a more self-aware approach.

Practice 9: Thinking Before You Speak

This is one that you will start to notice follows through with the deep listening.

How many times do you think before you speak?

Chances are, not all that much.

But, if you're someone that's struggling with their relationship or with their partner, sometimes, it's not on them, but it's on you. Thinking before you speak is a mindfulness skill and something that you need to begin practicing.

This can be harnessed through the power of mindfulness meditation, where you sit down, close your eyes, and just be there and breathe, letting all of the intrusive thoughts and actions get acknowledged, but you're not at the effect of them.

But how do you apply this to life?

Well, let's talk about how you can become aware of thinking before you speak, so you're not hurting yourself in the process.

1. First, become aware of yourself through mindfulness meditation

2. Once there, think about the conversations you've had. In how many have you actively thought before you spoke

3. If you notice that you don't, figure out why that is. Look at the reasoning behind it, and acknowledge it, but work on making it go away

4. Don't let it overtake you, but instead, start to focus on what you can do to help build a better process of thinking before you speak, such as taking a moment to collect your thoughts before you talk to others.

5. The next time you speak to your partner, wait a moment before you speak, and don't anticipate the next thought while they talk.

6. Practice deep listening as you listen to your partner. This will help curb thinking before you speak.

A big part of controlling this is well, being mindful. Once you're aware and mindful of what's going on, then you'll begin to notice that it's much easier for you to build awareness over time. So, don't be afraid to do that, but instead, become aware of what you're doing, so others can have a healthier mindset as well.

Practice 10: Loving-Kindness Writing Meditation

How much love do you send out to people sometimes? Is the reason why you're struggling with relationships because of your own lack of love for others? This can happen, and sometimes, the best thing to do is work on sending love and kindness out to others.

But, how do you do that? Well, fear not, because here, I'll tell you the steps that you need to take. It'll only take about 15 minutes of your time, but you can build more love, and more kindness than ever before with this…

1. To begin, sit comfortably with your feet on the floor and your spine straight, and relax your whole body with your eyes closed the entire time.

2. Breathe in first, and then breathe out. From here, think of someone you love very much, such as your partner. Imagine that person right next to you, sending their love towards you, wanting you to be happy, and safe.

3. From here, you should feel these wishes, and then repeat this with another person that wishes you well, and feel that too

4. From there, imagine everyone who has loved you, and picture all of them sending your happiness and wishes to one

another. Feel those wishes on every side as they flow inwards towards you.

5. Next, send that out to others, and first begin with the person right next to you, such as your partner, and send that love out first. Remember, you should wish them happiness.

6. Continue by focusing on the next person that you thought of, and wish for them to live with happiness, and ease.

7. From there, have another person in your life that you love, such as friends and relatives, and send these same wishes to them.

8. Send this to neutral people currently such as those you don't know, or those that you don't have feelings for, and wish them a good life.

9. Do this with another neutral person and wish them happiness and goodness in life.

10. Finally, expand this and envision your entire world in a ball in front of you, and send love and happiness to this as well, and wish for this.

11. Do this three times, breathe in, and then breathe out. You should notice your mind state once you're finished and when you're ready, open up your eyes.

This is a wonderful way to better understand the love that others have and can help you become more loving towards others. Most people don't even realize how hard it can be to feel love, especially in a world that very is cruel and doesn't love others. But this meditation can help with this and becoming mindful of everything that's happening is incredibly important.

Practice 11: Mindfulness of Physical Actions

Finally, let's take a moment to be mindful of physical actions. Do you ever think about how mindful you are of your partner's kisses, of their cuddles and hugs, or their intimacy? If the answer is no, then you need to start focusing on the mindfulness of this.

Commonly, one of the major issues people have in life is they're not mindful of the actions of others, which in turn causes problems with their relationships. That's because when you're not mindful of others, and your own actions, you act on automaton, with no feelings of love attached to this.

Becoming mindful of physical actions is a wonderful way to begin becoming more mindful of others.

To start, you need to do the following:

1. Pick an action that you typically are not mindful of such as brushing your teeth, showering, or even putting on clothes.

2. This time, start to feel and be aware of what's going on, such as the water running down your body, the feeling of the soap against your arms, the shampoo as it's massaged into your hair, the steam around you, the heat of the water, whatever it may be.

3. With brushing your teeth, become aware of the toothbrush hitting every single tooth as you begin to brush with this.

4. Continue to be mindful of these physical actions, so you can become more aware of the different natures of what's going on.

5. From here, the next time that you're cuddling with your partner, be aware of what it is that you're doing with them, and the way that they feel.

6. Become mindful of their heart rate, their breathing, the feeling of their kiss, their eye6 contact, whether their eyes are closed or even the environment. This will help you feel more aware of this.

7. You can also feel more appreciative and send out those feelings of gratitude. This will be helpful for everyone, and your partner will love it.

Physical actions are something you should become incredibly mindful of, because oftentimes, people aren't even aware of what they're doing. They don't realize the nuances of their partner, or what's going on, which can affect the way that things feel. Instead of just robotically going through the motions, start to build awareness of what's happening, so that in turn, you can be happy.

Mindfulness is one of the key aspects of building your relationship, and here, we told you why that is, and why it matters to be mindful of your actions and an awareness of others.

CHAPTER 4: USING EMOTIONAL INTELLIGENCE TO FIX YOUR RELATIONSHIP!

One aspect of relationships that people forget about is, of course, emotional intelligence. Emotional intelligence is one of the best ways to fix your relationship since it helps you understand your partner, and help you build awareness of what they're upset about. Being more aware of what's going on with your partner and reading the signs will help you prevent upsets from happening. But why does emotional intelligence matter? What can we do with it? Well, read on to find out!

What Is It?

Emotional intelligence at the core is the ability to manage and figure out not only your emotions but also, the emotions of another person. It's learning to regulate emotions so that you can create a better, more positive impact.

Typically, it includes three things:

• Your own personal awareness of your emotions

• The ability to hold onto those emotions and use them to create effects that help

• Managing emotions and helping others do the same

There isn't a test or scale for this such as for the general intelligence test, and oftentimes, it's not seen as a construct, but the way of describing your interpersonal skills. Emotional intelligence, however, has a lot of appeal amongst the masses, along with certain places. Employers have even made different intelligence tests to help determine emotion intelligence tests for people.

It is said that those with higher emotional intelligence would work better as a leader, or even someone in a senior position compared to a coworker.

How This Relates to Relationships

How this relates to relationships is simple. Those who are emotionally intelligent will be able to understand when they are emotional, whether positively or negatively, and they'll be able to manage said emotions.

This is crucial because people sometimes don't think before they speak, or they have an emotional outburst that's negative in response. If you're sensitive to the emotional signals, you'll be able to handle other people's emotions better, and you can be a better partner to the one that you care about.

Lots of times, people in romantic relationships will get emotional towards their partner, and they'll try very hard to keep everything together, but outbursts happen, anger strikes, and everyone is upset. Sometimes, your relationship might suffer due to the negative emotions you're experiencing, and that's one of the reasons why emotional intelligence is so important.

With emotional intelligence, you'll be able to talk a lot more to your partner about your thoughts, and you'll be able to handle all of the emotions that you have going on, without upsetting the other people around you. Wouldn't it be nice to say to others what is going on, without them getting mad, or if you notice your partner is upset, you handle it right away?

That's the real beauty of emotional intelligence.

With emotional intelligence, you can read your partner like a book, which can be immensely helpful. Lots of people who utilize this will begin to realize that it's okay to do this, since being able to read your partner and understand them will help in those trying times. You'll be able to, with all of your abilities and understandings, create a much more positive and happier life between both of you.

It also prevents you from getting worked up when things go sour. Have you ever dealt with your partner doing things that bothered you, to the point where you yelled at them, said something snarky and rude, and then later on you cool down? After some time, you realize the issue was so small you didn't need to make that much of a scene? Well, welcome to improper emotional intelligence. These are all signs of that, and often, if you boost this, you'll realize that you're fighting less, and building a better relationship with your partner.

You Understand the Consequences Better

For many people, high emotional intelligence lets you read what the other person is doing. This is a big part of learning to read and understand others. Sometimes, people who are not very forward emotionally can be hard to read, but you start to learn to read the signs, whether it is the way their eyes are downcast, or whether or not they're tensing and clenching their fingers.

From here, you can regulate your own emotions, and if you're frustrated, you hold that back, so you don't get mad at your partner. This is also holding yourself together even in the trying times. Sadness is something you can work to regulate better too.

This isn't turning you into a robot, not at all. It's learning how to regulate your own personal emotions so you don't need to worry others. This is incredibly important, and you'll be able to build more awareness of your thoughts as well as the ability to decrease your emotional power. You'll be able to handle the conflicts that come around and build it better.

With emotional intelligence, you build connections too. People understand that their words have power, that their emotions can affect situations. Negative emotions are contagious, like a disease, but, with the right understanding, and the right wellness you'll be able to build a much better, and more understanding situation not just for the arguments at hand, but also for your future.

A lot of people wonder how they can build emotional intelligence, how they can do it without harming others, well, the solution is in the next section, where I'll give you four practices that you can do in just 25 minutes a day, and from there, you'll be able to get a better understanding and grasp on the situation at hand, so you're happier about life as well. Once you learn to focus on this, you'll realize that it's possible.

Remember, this isn't going to be easy, but you'll start to realize that the way your thoughts connect can be a big part of how you experience emotions. If you have negative thoughts, you can learn to understand them, and make them go away. Of course, this takes practice, but it's possible.

Emotional intelligence is a vital skill, and you learned here how it can affect relationships for the better.

CHAPTER 5: EMOTIONAL INTELLIGENCE RELATIONSHIP PRACTICES

This section will tell you how you can build emotional intelligence for you, and your partner. It can be hard to do, but it's worth it, and it's certainly something you can improve with just a little bit of practice.

Practice 12: How and When to Use Emotional Intelligence

Learning how to use emotional intelligence comes down to

many different parts. There are a few things that you can do, and some different ways to help you build emotional intelligence. You need to understand the how, and the when to use this. You can do so by reading your own emotions, and also learning to understand your emotions a bit better.

Here, we'll give you a few ways you can learn how to use your emotional intelligence.

When Is It Best?

The answer is learning during a situation that is tumultuous. You should learn the emotions that you're having all the time. For a moment, close your eyes, and for a second, think about the emotions that you have. This can be what you're feeling, and what you're experiencing.

To understand when to use emotional intelligence, one of the best ways to do it is to name your emotions.

How do you do that? Well, try using the following:

1. The next time an emotion comes through, stop for a second

2. Look at the emotion, and from there, name what it is, whether it is anger, sadness, or whatever

3. Take a moment and stop and understand that it's a negative emotion, and it can be regulated

4. Sometimes, you can say this out loud as well, and it will help you with the distancing of the emotions. However, you'll want to use the third person with this one

This is good to use when you feel frustrated, and we'll discuss how you can apply emotional intelligence to anger later on.

Be the Fog!

This is another good emotional intelligence exercise. This might sound weird, but this is a good personal emotional intelligence practice to use, especially if you're receiving criticism, or suggestions on what to change.

Human beings aren't good at accepting criticism, and sometimes, one of the best practices to learn to modulate your emotions during arguments is to act like a fog.

The concept is that you're becoming a fog in a sense, where if someone throws stuff at you, you are like a fog, where it won't hurt you, but instead, you let it just get absorbed without throwing it back.

How do you do this? Well, the best way to accomplish this is to practice the following:

1. Someone throws a criticism at you

2. Instead of getting worked up or fighting, just accept it

3. From there, you just let it get said again and again

Remember, you don't have to believe this, but instead, it will disarm the emotions that are there, and it will stop the criticism. But you have to do this without emotional attachment either, which is crucial, because lots of people tend to do things without the emotions detached but creating a more detached outlook to things is so helpful, and it will help with regulating all of the emotions you're feeling.

Observing Your Thoughts

This is another personal emotional intelligence practice that will be helpful. It can be tough, but it will help you become mindful. In a sense, this is a mindfulness activity, and it is essential for you to understand yourself.

You should learn how to observe not just your thoughts, but also what will help with the actions at hand.

To observe your thoughts better, you do the following:

1. This is something you can do throughout the day. Every time you have a thought, look at the way that you feel

2. Once you begin to notice the way your thoughts connect to one another, think about the thoughts that cause negative emotions

3. Learn to understand which thoughts will cause negative emotions

4. From here, become mindful, and acknowledge that those thoughts make you feel this way

5. Tell yourself you're not going to give power to those thoughts

6. Instead, you keep your thoughts positive, since they keep a positive response

This is a great way to become more proactive with these issues. If you notice that you're negative when thinking about something, then don't try to get worked up in the emotions there, and instead, focus on the positive actions that will reduce the conflicts and instances.

You need to know what interactions make these come about too. Sometimes, if you know a meeting is going to be hard on you, and it's going to cause those negative thoughts, then you should prepare yourself mentally. Practice some mindfulness and utilize mindful breathing to help you relax. If you're going to discuss a situation with your partner that's hard for you to deal with, know what will trigger that, and what will help you build better emotional intelligence with the person.

Increasing Self-Awareness

Finally, let's talk about increasing self-awareness. You need a stack of some index cards, and some time by yourself. To practice this, you should start by asking yourself, how you feel. Chances are, you'll say that you're fine.

Sometimes, you may then ask yourself if it's easy to talk about the feelings, what makes it hard, and if you shift your feelings about. Write this down on a piece of paper. This will bring forth awareness of your feelings.

Next, you need to write down how understanding human emotions, not just within yourself but also within others, is important, and how it helps with regulating your feelings. From here, think about your emotions, write them down. From there, you should pick up an emotion and finally be able to explain the emotion to yourself.

From here, once you've looked at the emotion, you'll begin to realize that you can come up with emotions, and from there, you'll start to realize it's easy to do this, and you can see how you can switch to these emotions as needed.

Once you have mastered this, you can practice it with your partner, the next time there is conflict, remember how easy it is for you to switch emotions from one aspect to another, and work on building better emotional intelligence in this regard. That way, you don't have to obsess over this, and instead, know for a fact how you can regulate your emotional intelligence.

The simple answer is emotional intelligence can be used at all points of time, but the more complex answer is you should use emotional intelligence when you feel it's best to regulate your emotions, and you know it'll create conflict. That way, you can prevent the worst from happening, and you'll be able to build a better, happier life with the person that you love.

Practice 13: The Art of Reading Your Partner

Reading your partner is the next step with partners, they can be hard to read. But, with the right ideas, and the right understanding, you'll be able to build a better awareness of what your partner is going through.

If you notice that they are angry, for example, is it right to respond with anger? Of course not! But if you don't realize that they are angry, and you're all caught up in your own emotions, you're going to struggle with being happy. That's why, reading your partner is so essential, and here, we'll discuss how you can read your partner better.

Look at Their Body Language

This is important, and it's pretty obvious, but one of the best ways to understand and read your partner is to look at their body language.

For example, when they're angry, do they clench their fists? Do they tend to dart their eyes around, or do they focus on you? If you can see that, you'll know their emotions. You'll be able to look at the way their body starts to respond.

To practice this, begin with the following:

1. Next time you have an interaction, look at their eyes. If they're darting about, they're fearful. If they're super focused and serious, they are angry. If you notice they're relaxed, with no furrowed brows, then they're neutral in emotions. If their eyes are widened, they're surprised.

2. After, notice their breathing. Is it labored? If so, then it may be they're angry about something. If you notice it's going faster, almost paniclike, they're anxious about something. If you notice it's even, they're neutral.

3. Noe, look at facial expressions. These are obvious, but they can tell you certain things. However, some people are bad with

expressing emotions, and oftentimes, their anger might be mistaken for something else.

4. From here, look down at their body. Do you see tension Or are they relaxed? If they're tense, you can sense some anger or emotional turmoil there.

5. Take it all in, and spend a moment processing it. If they're criticizing you, instead of getting triggered and upset, maybe spend a moment just observing the emotions, and figuring out how to respond to this .

This is good to practice because reading your partner can be hard to do, but with the right mindset and ideas, it will help.

Make Eye Contact

This might be strange, but the practice of making eye contact is a wonderful way to build emotional intelligence not just in yourself, but in others too, and it's an obvious means of reading your partner.

Did you know humans don't make eye contact very well? It's a shame, but it's a problem lots of people have when they talk to their partners because they think the other person is ignoring them. But, making eye contact will help offset those negative emotions, and make you feel much better as well.

How do you improve your eye contact? Well, follow the steps below:

1. Next time you speak to your partner, even if it's just saying hello, look at them

2. Focus on their face, but don't overly focus.

3. Continue to do this throughout the day, without darting eyes.

4. From here, the next time there is an upset between both of you, you can build a better understanding by using eye contact.

5. Continue to work on eye contact, because it's a practice most of us shy away from.

Eye contact is one of the best ways to read your partner, and it can help you build a better understanding of what is going on emotionally in your partner too.

Ask Them How They're Feeling

This is another kind of obvious one, but did you know that sometimes the key to dispelling situations that are terse is to just ask them how they're feeling?

This might seem silly, but asking someone how they're feeling will help them realize and recognize their emotions. Plus, if your partner is the type that's hard to read in one way or another, this is one of the simplest practices to engage in.

So how do you do it without sounding weird? Well, you can just outright ask them what's going on, or even how they're feeling, and they can respond appropriately, but other times, it might be a little harder for them to explain it, and you might need to goad them a little bit.

The next time you notice a situation with questionable emotions in it, do the following:

1. Literally ask them how they're doing.

2. Have them explain it.

3. If you notice they get hostile or say "what are you thinking" just ask them how they're feeling.

4. Get them to explain it.

5. Have them explain their situation, and you'll notice it starts to dispel.

You'd be surprised at how effective this works. People are pretty easy to read with their body language, yes but getting your partner to recognize their emotions will build awareness and understanding of things, and in turn, help to build a better awareness of what it is that you're going through.

Practice 14: Anger Management and How to Beat It

Let's take a moment to talk about anger. Anger is an emotion. It's an emotion we all struggle with. If you're someone who has anger management issues, emotional intelligence on your own part is very important for you to learn. Here, we'll give you simple practices and practical tips that will assist you with beating anger and helping to manage it.

Wait a Minute Before Speaking

You've heard of thinking before you speak, right? That's a common practice that can help you immensely in learning to regulate your emotions. Thinking before you speak, understanding your emotions at hand, and from here, waiting a second before you respond can prevent reactionary measures.

This is hard, I understand this, but one thing you can use to stop yourself immediately, is, of course, breathing meditation.

How do you do this? Well, use the following practice:

1. The next time there is an upset, spend a moment just in silence, processing everything

2. Think about what you're going to say next, even if you notice that there is a negative emotion there

3. Figure out a thought that's connected to a positive emotion

4. Speak that, but always wait a moment

This is hard, but it can help with regulating the emotional turmoil you're going through, and help you to process the emotions at hand.

Don't be Afraid to Ask for a Minute To Cool Down

Now, I will say this one is critical if the emotions are too much, and you feel this. This can be very important for you to learn, because lots of times, people don't spend that extra moment cooling down, and in turn, they continue to get upset, and they just emotionally wail on their partner, creating chaos and illogical situations.

So how do you learn to ask for a minute to cool down? Well,

the simplest way is to know your triggers and know what will make you upset.

Knowing your triggers and figuring them out so that you know when you need to take a break is crucial. Triggers are often reduced to something that makes a person "weak" in our society, but we all have triggers. They're the buttons that get pressed that upset up.

If you're trying to resolve situations with another person, you need to learn your triggers and learn when it's best to step back. This can be hard, and I understand that, but learning what they are, and then taking a moment to cool down, and communicating that as well, will change the game.

How do you do this? Well, practice the following:

1. First, sit down and learn your triggers, understanding what makes you tick, and what makes you upset.

2. When you recognize these triggers, start to meditate on them, and when they come up, along with the issues or negative thoughts that come with this, learn to acknowledge them.

3. The next time you have a situation that sets you off, you can recognize this, and from there, if it becomes too much, start to communicate to your partner that you're upset.

4. From there, spend some time away to cool down before you continue.

5. If it's something you will need to face that upsets you, the best thing to do in that regard, is, of course, take the emotions

that are with those thoughts, and recognize them, thinking about them for a moment, and then speaking.

Anger is very hard to deal with but trying this might be the best option for you.

Recognize Your Patterns

Did you know that we all have patterns of how we respond to situations? Yes, that's right, our brains have a natural stimulus-response mechanism to some of the different situations that are there. Everyone follows patterns, and for many of us if we have a pattern that works, we keep it and if it doesn't, we scrap it.

The best way to manage your own anger is to look at your patterns and recognize them. Remember, knowing is half the battle, and recognizing how you respond to situations is crucial.

How do you do that though? Well, read below for some solutions to recognizing your own patterns of behavior.

1. First, sit down and look at your emotions

2. Take the negative emotion. Start to write what you do when you're angry. For example, if you're the type who bottles it up, write down that you bottle that emotion up till you explode.

3. Now, that's obviously not a healthy behavioral pattern. You need to sit down and look at it rationally to figure out when you do that. From here, start to recognize the source of this.

4. Write down actionable steps to get past this, and bring forth a much better, healthier understanding of not just yourself, but also the other person.

5. Next time you're angry, recognize this pattern, or next time you're upset, recognize the pattern, so you can learn to change this.

This is also a good point in time to understand the buildup before the trigger. Remember, we all have triggers and we all have buildups too. There is always something that's there, building itself up before you get fully triggered by the situation. Emotions are essentially the way that we respond to different thoughts and upsets. Oftentimes, if we can recognize the buildup, and check in when the buildup happens, we'll be much happier, and we can see the buildup that comes with this as well.

Self check-ins are essential, and you can use this as well. Literally, the process is, if you're having a rough day, check in with yourself, and find out how you're doing. This is very important for learning to beat these emotions and helping with understanding the issues that you're struggling with.

For many, understanding anger issues involves recognition, and sometimes, emotional intelligence is necessary for building and understanding your issues as well.

Can You Respond with Kindness?

This is another practice you can use to help with beating anger issues. This is a good way for you to learn how to understand your own anger and how to respond with kindness.

For many, in our relationships, we tend to act irrationally, and sometimes that first emotion we pick is not happiness or kindness, it's anger. How many times have you irrationally responded to a situation that you could've easily just responded to with kindness? Kindness is amazing because it's almost like a disarming device that can be used to stop the problems that you have going on.

Do you know the phrase killing with kindness? Well, basically that's what you're doing here.

The general idea behind this is to kill the issue with kindness. Kindness can go a long way, and it can change how you respond to issues at hand. For many people, responding with kindness rather than anger isn't easy though, and there are many different problems that come about because of it. Usually, it's due to your own stubbornness, but one of the best things you can do is learn to be kinder. This is a type of emotional intelligence technique that can diffuse those situations that are hard to deal with, so you're happier.

How do you do this though? Well, the steps for this include the following:

1. Work on practicing loving-kindness meditation on the regular, so you can work on improving the way you send out love to others.

2. Next, you need to start being kinder. Write down different ways you can be kinder to others.

3. From here, figure out actionable solutions that allow you to be kinder.

4. The next time you and your partner have an argument, be kind. Even if it's something small, such as saying thanks, acknowledging your faults, or whatever it takes, most times it will diffuse the situation.

5. Work on trying to implement kindness into your everyday life, because it will help with building and maintaining healthier relationships with yourself, and with others too.

Anger is an emotion we all deal with, but remember, all of the negativity can be killed with kindness. Even in those situations where you don't think it would work, trust me, it does work. Learning to recognize that kindness is a powerful tool is crucial, and you should definitely work on beating this as well.

The Myth of Bad Emotions

Did you know that sometimes the reason we are antagonistic with our emotions is cause we think about them as bad? Not every semblance of anger is terrible, and not every feeling of grief is bad? At the end of the day, emotions are essentially pieces of data that exist to help us overcome the trials of life. Being able to overcome the mindset that good and bad emotions exist will help us with improving the way we handle emotions.

This is where emotional regulation comes in. Being able to regulate your emotions, and being able to think before you speak, or even just recognize when you are angry, you'll be able to make the emotions an ally, rather than an enemy.

This is something lots deal with on a regular basis. They think being mad is terrible, but if you notice when you are angry, and the results of this, you'll be able to understand your emotions, and recognize good along with the fact that bad emotions aren't necessarily the case. Emotions are used to send responses and messages, such as fear focusing on what we're looking at, such as a threat, and it motivates us to protect. Sadness helps us recognize the person that we care about. If you are looking to improve your emotional intelligence, you've got to stop fighting those emotions.

This isn't easy though, as you'll soon realize. But sometimes if you sit down, take a deep breath, and recognize these emotions, you'll be incredibly liberated, and it can help with building an understanding.

Emotions are powerful yes but learning to recognize them is a key part of emotional intelligence, and you should stop fighting the fight that's there.

Practice 15: Providing Logical Solutions to Issues at Hand

Now, one of the best ways to utilize emotional intelligence is of course to provide logical solutions to the arguments that are transpiring. This should be obvious, but lots of times the reason why couples don't do this is because they're obsessed with being right, with the irrational thoughts taking over, and they exhibit bad behaviors that reduce their emotional intelligence. But how can you use emotional intelligence to provide logical solutions? I'll give you the exact practice below, and what you need to do.

Take Turns Talking

One of the best ways to regulate emotions during arguments or upsets is to take turns talking. Interruptions will just keep the fires burning, and it's very important to understand that, if you're struggling to provide logical solutions to the issues at hand, you need to learn how to take turns talking.

Arguments typically end in the way they begin. That's why taking things slow and arguing slowly will help with making difficult conversations easier.

Why is it important to take it slow? Well, it allows you to emotionally regulate too! That's because it alerts you do the following:

• Read your partner's body language

• From here, deeply listen to what they're saying

• Get a grasp on what's going on without the emotions attached to it

• Respectfully respond

How many times do you respectfully respond to a conversation? Chances are you don't. Chances are, this is great for the two of you because if you sit down and be quiet while the other speaks, you'll realize it's much easier to have a conversation. You can emotionally regulate and sit down and listen.

This is a great way to diffuse arguments too. If you both agree to sit down and listen, you'll realize it's much easier to provide the logical solutions to the outcomes too.

Provide Multiple Solutions

One of the problems with arguments and situations that are terse is that they tend to have this effect that only one solution is correct, a "my way or the highway" sort of approach. But, if you sit down and both provide solutions, working towards a compromise, you'll realize it will help with an actual solution, instead of just floundering about trying to figure out how you can build a solution on an already rocky surface.

How you do this is simple. What you do is the following:

1. First, discuss the problem together

2. Next, say that you have a solution, but it doesn't have to be yours

3. Say your solution

4. Ask your partner if they have a solution

5. If they do, let them speak, and respectfully listen

6. If they don't, ask if they want to figure this out at a different point in time, or talk about it after thinking over

7. If they say yes, then give it time, and come back to it

8. Let them say their solution and from there work to meet a middle ground

9. Both of you explain the pros and cons logically behind this, and instead of getting upset, figure out solutions.

Agreed, this does take longer, but if you start to approach it in this regard, you'll realize it's much easier to handle these stressful relationships.

Don't Use Name-Calling or other Insults

This one should be obvious, but you're never going to get anywhere if the two of you are using schoolyard names that are mean towards the other person. This one should be a given, but in the heat of the moment, you'll say things you don't mean.

If you want to provide logical solutions, the two of you need to sit down and explain yourselves. If you feel like saying something mean, recognize that, and acknowledge that thought, but don't say it. Don't let it have power, but instead, focus on the positive, like figuring out a solution. Really figure out how you can benefit from solving this fight.

This is a big one, because insults get you nowhere, trust me on this. They will definitely create nothing but issues, and if you're trying to put together a logical solution, you're going to create chaos if you call one another names.

Compromise!

Now, I'm not saying you should sit down and just take what your partner says at face value. That's one way to get upset with one another, but the logical solution to arguments is to set up compromises.

Compromises will change the game completely. If you're compromising, you'll realize that it's much easier for the two of you to talk out the issues, and if there is a solution, it'll be more logical.

Now, I'm not saying this is going to make you happy, but part of a relationship is seeing what the other person is thinking about and working on a logical solution to this. That way, they'll feel acknowledged, and the two of you can come to a middle ground, understanding one another and building a better relationship.

How do you get better at compromising? Well, it does involve a little bit of emotional regulation to help bring forth a sound argument and solution.

1. First and foremost, think about the emotions that arise when you compromise.

2. Recognize them, and realize that they don't have to have that power over you.

3. From here, during the argument or discussion, suggest compromising.

4. Bring forth different perspectives, saying yours, and from there having the person say theirs.

5. Both of you agree on which part of this the two of you can budge a little bit on. For example, if you're arguing about finances, maybe you can agree not to go shopping as much, and they can agree to unsubscribe from one TV service.

6. From here, both of you put together a line of agreement that lets you both see that the other person has their own side, and you do care about both. Explain that you want to build a better response from this.

For many people, compromises are hard. It isn't easy to deal with at times, and the reality is that people don't like to fight, but they get into arguments because the other person has their own viewpoint and you have yours. But you need to listen to different perspectives. Having your own and only your own, and an echo chamber in response will only make both of you upset, and it's why some people feel like their partner doesn't care. That's why, if you're struggling with your relationship, figure out where you're not being heard, and work on trying to build a better relationship with one another.

Again, this is also recognizing and handling emotions, and understanding the other person in a logical manner. Emotional intelligence is very important. It can help you understand anger, and it is definitely helpful for both of you to sit down and figure out for yourself what you need to get done, and what will help both of you do better in life.

Remember, you can always be better, and by mastering emotional intelligence, it's totally possible.

CHAPTER 6: ESTABLISHING EMOTIONAL INTIMACY

Emotional intimacy is something that's missing in many relationships. Sometimes, the reason why you're struggling with your relationship and/or with your partner isn't just the arguments, it's the lack of intimacy on an emotional level.

Sure, you may have amazing physical intimacy, and that's

great, but if you're lacking in the emotional intimacy department, you'll start to realize there are issues in your relationship.

Couples experience this more often than they think, which is why establishing emotional intimacy, and learning how to do so with the right practices is crucial.

First, we'll discuss what emotional intimacy is, and why it's important to establish emotional intimacy with the person you love.

So, What Is It?

At the core, emotional intimacy is the closeness between you and your partner in terms of your emotions and connections. Emotional intimacy is different from physical intimacy.

We're all familiar with physical intimacy in some way, shape or form especially when it comes to sex, or even just kissing and cuddling. But emotional intimacy does involve showcasing that you're there for your partner, that you can feel trust and communication between both of you. It builds that connection that lets you see into the soul of the partner, and it's where the hopes and dreams come from, along with the fears, concerns, and worries. This in turn, will let you understand your partner on a deeper level.

Relationships that don't have this have low levels of trust, communication, hidden feelings, and secrets.

This is where the fear that your spouse is cheating on you

comes from, or a wave of anger because your partner has secrets, or they're doing something wrong. Sometimes, if you feel distant from the person you love, this is because you're not emotionally intimate with your partner.

Now, emotional intimacy is crucial for many reasons, but here's the scary thing: our society doesn't have it in many cases. Lots of relationships don't develop it initially, or over time, you lose it. Both partners do build intimacy on a sexual level, and for many, we're always worried about sex on a personal level. Yes, sex is an essential part of intimacy, but emotional intimacy is just as important, if not more important than physical intimacy.

You can have sex with your partner and it's wonderful, but if you feel like you're living or married to a total stranger, is it worth it? Do you feel happy? I'm going to be honest with you, chances are that isn't the case.

Emotional intimacy is just as important as the physical aspects, and people don't recognize this issue until it's too late, when you think your partner is cheating, you have a blowup, and you're both upset.

Why This Matters

I explained in detail why our society is struggling because of a lack of emotional intimacy, but I'm going to break it down for you further.

Emotional intimacy is something most couples lack. You may not even realize that this is happening, until you start to realize that you're both incredibly distanced from one another.

Have you ever felt like your partner wasn't available, or maybe they just don't seem to care? That's a prime example of this, and, it doesn't get seen until the divorce papers are in place, and everything is in shambles.

Women have been blindsided by their husband suddenly leaving their marriages, and vice versa. That's a normal problem, and it's a big issue for couples. But, upon further inspection, sometimes you can notice the signs.

Being distanced emotionally, feeling like your partner doesn't give a damn, all of these are examples of a lack of emotional intimacy in the marriage that you have. If you're not careful, you're going to fall into this trap.

Now, emotional intimacy may already be lacking in your marriage. This commonly happens, but the nice thing about emotional intimacy is that you can easily deepen the connection.

In our world, electronics dominate the floor. On many occasions you'll notice a couple together, where they're both on their phones, rarely talking to each other. That doesn't mean they're completely emotionally uninvolved. Some people use their phones as a crutch. But if you notice they never spend time together, or whenever they do, they are just on their phones glued to a screen, that's a sign of a much bigger, more worrisome issue. If there is a lack of emotional intimacy though, spending time together can make a difference.

The beauty of emotional intimacy is that it's probably one of the easiest practices to employ, but it can be a challenge especially if you and your partner have strange schedules, or maybe your time together is very lacking. However, that means it's even more critical to get on this, to fix the issue before it gets worse.

Now, these practices will go into great detail on each of these points and help you establish emotional intimacy between one another. Sometimes, the reason why you're not emotionally intimate with your partner is simply due to the fact that you're both separated. What I will say, is when you start to employ these practices, do put some time aside for this. Again, it doesn't have to be long. About thirty minutes is a good start, but some couples tend to find out that they like spending time with their partner and may spend more time on this one.

But, if you're ready to fix your marriage or relationship, then look at emotional intimacy or a lack thereof in it. This is the single most common reason as to why you're both unhappy, and just changing how the distance is between the two of you will change your life, and in turn, make it much better for you as well. So how do you do it? Well, read on to find out in the next few sections how you can increase this necessary part of you.

Practice 16: Emotional Needs — Both His and Hers

Understanding the emotional needs on both ends is incredibly important. Otherwise, if you don't know what your partner wants, they won't be happy.

This isn't just your needs either. It's your partner's. If you notice your partner is upset, then it'll only spiral both of you down the path of unhappiness.

Figuring this out does take time. You need to spend time learning about what the other person wants, and what they desire from a relationship of course.

Figuring this out is easier said than done though.

But, if the two of you talk it out, it'll make everything better in the relationship on multiple levels.

How do you talk out your emotional needs with the other person? There are a few things you can do to help rectify the problem.

First, on a personal level, you need to identify your own emotional needs. If you're not happy, you're going to suffer. To figure this out, do the following:

1. Sit down on your own, identify the places where you're happy in your relationship. It doesn't have to be anything in-depth.

2. From here, identify the actual issues you have with your relationship, and the emotional needs you feel stunted. Be descriptive of this.

3. At this point, figure out the exact steps that you need to take to get those emotional needs met, and where everything went wrong.

4. Figure out the plan to talk with your partner about their emotional needs.

At this point, you need to sit down with your partner, and work on establishing your emotional needs together. While it is good to pinpoint where the needs aren't being met, if you're not establishing the emotional needs on both ends, you won't get better.

How do you do this? Follow the practice below. It doesn't have to take long but working together will help you immensely.

1. First, encourage both of you to sit down, without any distractions or the link.

2. From here, talk about how you're feeling a lack of emotional connection, even something as simple as the two of you are distanced.

3. Talk to your partner and ask them if there is anything going on.

4. From there, let them talk, and let them get out what they need to say.

5. Talk to them about emotional needs and talk about the reality of the situation: that both of you have distanced yourself from one another.

6. Talk about how it makes you feel, how you don't like to feel distanced from him.

7. From there, talk about the emotional needs you'd like to meet, and the ones you need help establishing.

8. At this point, get them to talk about the emotional needs they feel are lacking.

9. Really let them get it out, and from there, once they've said everything, you should talk about how to get this back in place. If there was an argument that needed to be ironed out, talk about that, and from there, talk out your feelings.

10. Don't hold back when talking about this, because if you do hold yourself back, you're going to reduce the chances of a strong emotional connection.

11. Overcome the obstacles together by defining the problem in terms of emotional needs, and then from there, you can work together in order to eliminate the obstacle.

12. Plan out activities together to establish the emotional connection together

Emotional needs are very important. Understanding not just your own, but also your partner's is essential to success. For many couples, they lost that spark, and they lost that intimacy of the connection together. But, by bringing it back, by springing it forward and working together, you can build a better, more worthwhile life together, and you'll be able to, with this as well, create a happier life.

Remember, emotional needs are important to understand when working to construct better emotional intimacy, and for every relationship, it's super important. Don't neglect it, since it can ultimately help you figure out the problem and establish the solution to these issues in a correct manner.

Practice 17: Mastering Honesty and Openness

Honesty is the best policy, and it's something couples need to have.

One of the reasons why your relationship might be strained is because you're not open and honest with one another. But, for couples, by establishing an honest and open relationship together, you'll be much happier.

Think about it, when you tell your partner things, you feel good, right? Oftentimes, people don't realize how important honesty and openness is, and you need to understand that openness is something both of you needs to work on.

How can you be more honest though? Well, being transparent can be hard, but you need to learn how to be forthright with the words you want to say. But it can be a good way to practice both honesty, and openness between both of you.

What are some ways you can master honesty though with your partner? Well, do the following:

1. First, think about all of the things you haven't told your partner that they should probably know. Write them down.

2. At this point, write down why you haven't told your partner

about it. If it involves any infidelity and such, figure out how you can let them know the truth about it.

3. Look at the consequences: will it hurt you if you tell them.

4. In the instance of infidelity, you need to tell your partner, because otherwise, it's going to hurt them.

You should sit down and figure out every area you're not being honest in, and where you can get better with this. It can be hard, but the right mindset will help you with mastering it. At this point, it is good if you talk to your partner. How do you talk about this with them though? Well, why not try the steps listed below.

If you're looking to get more honest with your partner, consider the following:

1. First, figure out a place where both of you can talk freely without distractions.

2. From here, talk about how you want to be more open about things.

3. Tell your partner some of the things you haven't been open about.

4. Try to do this with as little emotional attachment as you can. That doesn't mean a lack of responsibility, but instead, it means being honest and working towards bettering yourself.

5. Next, have your partner tell you what's going on.

6. Both of you discuss why you wouldn't tell your partner

these things. Talk about why you've hidden this. It might sound strange, but it can help to shed some light on why you're both being aloof on the subject.

7. From here, work together in order to practice better open communication, and reaffirm that the two of you can work through everything together as needed, and get an establishment put in place for these conversations.

8. Both of you need to agree to have this type of openness, and once a week, sit down and just tell the other person what's going on, how you're feeling, and the like.

Remember, honesty isn't just being honest about what you've done or not done, it's also about how you feel. For example, if you feel sad about a lack of intimacy, you need to be honest with your partner, and tell them how you feel. This is good for both of you, and together you can work on being honest in this relationship.

Both of you need to master the practice of honesty, because it will help with improving your relationship, and build a better one. Part of the reason why couples struggle with their lives is due to a lack of honesty, so understand that it's incredibly important to do this, and remember that honesty is the best policy at the end of the day.

Practice 18: Intimate conversations—How and When to Have Them

One thing that will help you with having a better connection with your partner, and to build emotional intimacy, is to make sure that both of you have intimate conversations with one another. But, what's the best way to have these? After all, being emotionally intimate with a distinct partner can be quite hard. Well, here we'll teach you how to have these, such as what to say, and when you should have them.

In terms of when you need to make sure that you won't get interrupted by the other outside forces that are going on. For example, if you have kids, do this after they're put to bed or out of the house. If your partner has a work issue, you should let them focus on that, and from there, you should talk to them.

Some tips on when to have a conversation that's intimate include the following:

• Do it when it's quiet around you, and neither of you is distracted.

• Make sure to put all of the electronics away.

• If there is a personal issue that one of you needs to attend to, work on that first before you have this conversation.

• If needed, set a certain time of the week to sit down, be honest with one another, and have this type of conversation. For those who are busy, this is the best way to approach this.

Now, how do you have an intimate conversation like this? There are a few things that you need to do, and some steps to take into account include the following:

1. First, both of you need to establish a time when it's just the two of you, with no outside forces or other issues at hand.

2. You will need to be the one to initiate the conversation with them, since for many, if the other person hasn't by now, then they won't. First, tell them about what's going on, and how you feel, and then your partner will talk about this with you.

3. Don't be afraid to ask questions of your partner. You should always try to learn more about your partner. Never think that they will always be 100% known, because you'll never fully understand your partner, and that's where boredom sets in.

4. When having these conversations be vulnerable. Be willing to show yourself completely to the other person and establish who you are on a different level.

5. Work on trying to share secrets. This can be hard, I understand that, but if you truly do love and trust your partner, you'd be willing to tell them intimate secrets. Plus, if you tell your partner things, then they'll share the secrets back to you.

6. Touch each other while you talk. Hold hands, touch your partner's leg or back, or whatever, and just talk about your days with one another, and what's going on, and you'll start to realize that physically touching your partner is a great way to establish a deep connection.

7. If you're talking about anything heavy, let them know that you're there for them, and tell them that you're by their side, and you want to work together to move past them.

8. Let them know that you're grateful for them because this will help let them feel valuable in the relationship, helping to establish the gratitude that's necessary.

9. Work on having a practical conversation, but also consider some lovey-dovey and deep aspects. By working through the problems together, it can help.

10.End it by kissing and hugging one another. Remember, this is your partner. You love them and don't let them forget it. That way, it will make them feel wanted and valued as well.

Having intimate conversations can be scary, but by understanding one another, you'll be able to build a better, more rewarding relationship with them, and in turn, help to build trust and happiness with one another as well.

Practice 19: End-of-the-Day Communications and Why They Matter.

Do you talk to your partner at the end of the day? Do you ever ask them how their day went, and any problems they had?

If the answer to that is no, chances are there are going to be problems as a result of those words.

For many couples, conversations at the end of the day may not happen, but it does offer a wide variety of benefits. It can do the following for both of you:

• It lets you talk about your days together

• It lets you connect on an intimate level

- If there are any issues that you must discuss together, this is the way to do it

- You'll feel better and more refreshed

A good conversation at the end of the day allows you to work through any hurdles you ran into. Plus, the two of you can show intimacy before you go to bed, and both of you can go to bed in a better headspace.

Lots of times, the reasons why couples feel distanced is because they don't speak to their partner before they go to sleep. Whether it's due to different work schedules or what, having this lack of intimacy through end-of-the-day conversations can take a toll on you after a while. It's incredibly simple to do, and it doesn't have to take long either, but they can be longer conversations if you so desire.

How do you build better end-of-the-day conversations together? Well, consider trying the following plan, and see what will happen with this:

1. First, you both should establish a little bit of time to do this together, with as few distractions as possible. You could do this in bed.

2. Initiate the conversation, maybe by talking about your day, and how you want to tell your partner about your day more.

3. If your partner is open and willing, they'll listen, and provide their own insight too.

4. If you notice your partner is balking on this a bit, ask them if there was something bad in their day, and get them to talk.

5. Tell them that you had either a good day, or a rough day, and talk about it. Just vent about the issues that day.

6. Have your partner do the same.

7. At this point, talk about what you could do better, or the plan for tomorrow. Planning out your future endeavors can help you build a better, more intimate conversation with them.

8. Work together through any issues that transpire together, so that the two of you can work on building a better, more rewarding experience.

9. At the end of it, give one another a kiss, and you two can both say goodnight to one another and affirm that you love each other.

Saying this before bed is also good because you guys can get anything that's lingering in your head out in the open. You'd be surprised how helpful that can be. Getting it in the open will help you build a better and more intimate connection together so that both of you can have a better day tomorrow.

Plus, it's nice to find out how the other person's day was. Maybe there was something you could help them do better, and something that'll benefit them. It's worth trying, that's for sure.

With the right mindset and the right attitude, these conversations before you go to bed can help improve your relationships.

Practice 20: Doing Meaningful Activities Together

Meaningful activities are some of the best things you can do with your partner. By meaningful activities, we mean activities that allow you to foster good communication, and you can work together on different activities that can help build your communication skills and muster the courage to talk about anything that's needed.

For many couples, they fall into the trap of the mundane. While it might be fine initially, it starts to bring forth problems over time when you're trying to branch out and do something new. This also brings forth boredom and a strained relationship. So, what's the best way to combat that?

The answer is, of course, learning new activities, and building on these together!

What are some activities that are good for couples? Well, there are a few that are better than others, and some that might be downright silly, but sometimes, even those silly activities can provide a meaningful experience for both of you, and one way to practice emotional intimacy is to do something a bit off-the-wall and different.

Remember, variety is the spice of life, and sometimes, it's okay to try something a bit kooky and weird, and it's okay to be weird together.

What are some meaningful activities the two of you can do together? Well, why not consider the following:

• Go on a walk together.

• Learn a new hobby together.

• Work on a puzzle together, this also builds communication and you two can work together as a team.

• Try the other person's hobbies: this can be hard for some people, but one way to truly learn about your partner is to learn their hobbies.

• Go on a road trip, and this is a good way to help build a nice little relationship, and you two can learn even more about one another with a road trip.

• Start to have dinner together. You'd be surprised just how many couples don't do this, but this is one of the simplest activities to do together.

• Sit together comfortably in silence, maybe cuddling or next to one another. It is a good way to get comfortable in another person's presence, and it doesn't take a long time to build on this one.

• Cuddle together, maybe while watching a movie or even just talking to one another. It's the ultimate intimacy short of sex, and it's nice for the two of you together.

• If you both like to play video games, try playing a co-op game together. This lets you communicate with each other, and while it might be frustrating at first, it can help you to build a better connection. Plus, once you've beaten the boss, it can be a rewarding experience for both of you.

• Keep a notebook open in the kitchen and write some positive things for the other person. Whenever there is a disagreement, you should open up the book, and you two can remember how much you care and love each other. It's sweet, and a good way to dispel arguments, that's for sure.

• Do something spontaneous. For example, going on a trip together, maybe checking out a festival, maybe going to the park and spending time with one another, all of this will help you build a different plan and have a good time, without any issues.

• Work on your home: this is a good way to work together on different aspects of your space, and sometimes, a home improvement project is a wonderful way to build communication.

When it comes to these activities, sometimes you can plan them, sometimes not. If you're already in a relationship that's strained, try to plan it at least a little bit, so that it's not as hard on everyone else, but remember that it's okay to try new things together, to be weird together, and to have fun. When you're working on activities, it doesn't always have to be something you fully understand either, but instead, it can make it much better for the two of you to work on building up one another and building a deeper connection.

Practice 21: Make it Harder to Run Away

This is a bit hard to work on initially, but it involves working on building yourself up so you're a better person, but also working on standing up for yourself too.

Making it hard to run away from conversations is incredibly important. We will often try to avoid the inevitable, but if we continue to avoid certain situations, it'll make everything worse.

Have you ever tried to avoid a conversation with your partner? Not fun, right? Well, what about facing this, braving it, and actually doing something about it, instead of hiding in the shadows?

This is something that will help you, especially when you're having a rough time with establishing conversations, or also working through intimacy issues. But, one key part of emotional intimacy, is the bravery for standing up for what you want and having the courage to not run away.

For many people, those hard conversations are never easy for you to work with. They usually are avoided because of the following:

- You don't want to hurt your partner.

- You're scared of their reaction.

- It's better to hide, at least in your eyes.

But, is it all that better? It doesn't sound like it, and it isn't.

The best way to establish emotional intimacy with your partner is being honest and also making it hard to run away from these conversations.

But where do you begin? Well, for starters, you need to realize you have to have this conversation, or else your relationship will continue to stagnate, which isn't fun for anyone.

The one way to completely destroy intimacy is avoidance. People won't build a better relationship if they're distant, that's for sure.

You have to understand that the best way to tackle the problem is to actually face it. You will have to be vulnerable, yes, but the best thing to remember from that is that the other person will also be vulnerable too, and avoiding it will make it worse.

You want to make it harder to run away. I'm not saying you have to put up a giant wall or anything in the space physically, but you should be more aware of changes, and handle the conversation better between both of you. What you need to do is the following:

1. Have both of you establish a certain time when both of you can talk.

2. Initiate the conversations, even if it's difficult.

3. If your partner is balking on talking, tell them that you care, and you want to improve the health of the relationship, rather than avoid the discomfort that's there.

4. Have your partner, if they do try to run away, sit down, and insist that the two of you work it out.

5. If they're hesitant, also let them know how much you love them. That way, they can understand that you're not doing this to harm the relationship, but to do some good in the ordeal.

6. If they are hesitant to talk about it because they think you'll be mad, tell them that you need to have this conversation with them, so that they can continue to have a healthy relationship.

The end goal of this is to try and push the idea that they are needed, and that you care about them. I know it's hard, and I know that for some people it can be a troublesome activity, but for many, avoidance will make it worse. Don't reduce your own self-worth because you don't know how to handle this type of intimacy, but instead, you should try and, with the right mindset and ideas, have a good understanding of what you must do.

For many people, the right level of intimacy can benefit both of you, and by doing it correctly, you'll be able to prevent the worst from happening.

Make it harder to run away by being brave, but not mean about it. Also, make sure that you have it planned out how you're going to make this work, and how you're going to handle this type of confrontation. It will benefit you if you're smart and if you know what you're doing as you talk to them.

Practice 22: Shaking Up the Routine

One big way to increase emotional intimacy is to shake up the routine.

How many times have you tried to do something different, something that's different from the generalized routine that you have in place? It can be a bit of a hard road to travel, but understanding what your routine is, and then shaking it up, will change the relationship for the better.

Boredom and mediocrity are only going to make the relationship boring. How many times have you felt "bored" doing the same thing over and over again? It isn't that your partner is boring, but you just feel bored doing the same thing.

The changes to your routine will make things much easier, and you'll realize that sometimes, you can find out new and fun activities to do together.

But, how do you shake up the routine? What can you do? Well, here are a few steps that you can take to help make changes to your routine so that it's not the same thing over and over again.

1. Next time they have to take care of a chore that you don't like doing, you should say that you'll do it.

2. Come with them whenever they do something by themselves. If your partner likes to golf, maybe tag along, when normally you'd just let them go alone.

3. Get curious about what your partner is doing, and actively ask questions that you normally wouldn't.

4. Plan the dates, don't let your partner plan them this time around.

5. Surprise them with their favorite meal, which they may or may not normally ask for.

6. Watch a movie that they love but you can't stand while you cuddle with them.

7. Learn about their interests, and get curious about it, even if you don't care all that much about it initially.

8. From here, do the chores, or do something that normally your partner has to nag you about

These are all simple little things, it involves just opening your heart a tiny bit, and being silly to understand and try your best at making them happy. When you do these, don't also show any protest, but instead act as if you legitimately care about what they're doing, and what they are into. You'd be surprised at the difference this will make in your relationship.

Lots of times, shaking up the routine might be a bit awkward at first. This can happen especially if you notice your partner is a bit different or odd with their hobbies, but with the right understanding, and the right attitude, you'll be able to get a feel for what your partner enjoys, and this is a big intimacy booster.

Plus, there's always the chance that you'll learn about something you may not normally care about.

Sometimes, variety is the spice of life, and you should

consider shaking up your current routines and do something different. That way, the next time you feel bored, you have choices on what you can do.

For many people, emotional intimacy is one of the easiest ways to fix your relationship. That's because it's something that you can put back in without too much trouble. If you feel like something is lacking in your relationship, chances are it's your own sheer lack of emotional intimacy that you have, or you don't have. If you feel like something is lacking, or if you need a little bit of a boost, this is a great way to incorporate that into this, and in turn, can help you build that relationship of your dreams.

CHAPTER 7: SPICING UP YOUR SEX LIFE WITH SEXUAL INTELLIGENCE

Let's talk about sex. Spicing up your sex life can help your relationship immensely. While sex isn't the only thing in a relationship, it can be a focal part of it.

One problem with some people is they get bored. It isn't like they want to feel that way, but if you've had sex with your partner a few times, you probably know what they like.

But sometimes, the problem with one's sex life isn't that they don't know, it's that they already know what will happen, and what's going to happen next. This can spell boredom for both of you. If you notice that it's starting to feel that way, one of the best ways to spice it up is sexual intelligence. How do you do that?

Well, you're about to find out. Here, you'll learn all about sexual intelligence, and how to practice it with these exercises here.

What is Sexual Intelligence

Sexual intelligence is understanding the needs of your partner and working to meet them.

What that means at the core, is knowing what your partner likes, and having the decency to showcase that.

For a lot of people, they think they're doing something their partner likes when in reality, it isn't something they enjoy. For example, there's the whole joke about men not knowing what women like in bed and only care about their own needs.

However, sometimes that is misinterpreted as such, when in reality the other person doesn't know.

The human body is a bit strange, and sometimes, experimenting and trying something new isn't easy. That's because, people tend to think sex is a one-stop thing, and only can be done a certain way. But, in reality, sexual fulfillment is something people should work towards with their partner, and sexual intelligence can help.

Sexual intelligence involves reading what your partner is feeling in bed, and also knowing what they like, where they like it. It's important that couples learn how to exhibit this, since oftentimes, it's swept under the rug. In the real world, it's a very important aspect for you and your partner to work on.

I understand it can be hard initially because let's face it, sex talk can be awkward between people if they normally don't discuss it, but affection, sexual fulfillment, and the like are so important to many relationships that learning what the other person likes in bed is essential to your happiness.

How can you learn about this? Read below to find some of the best practices out there.

Practice 23: Affection and Sexual Fulfillment — How to Get It

So how do you get it? There are a few things you can do in order to achieve sexual fulfillment and affection. Below, we'll offer a few tips, and some practices to get used to when you're trying to get sexual fulfillment.

Talk It Out!

One of the easiest ways to improve your sexual fulfillment and affection is to talk it out. Simply sit down and talk to the other person. Some of the steps you can utilize on this point include the following:

1. Initiate the conversation.

2. Bring up a new and cool technique to try, since that can help with talking it out.

3. Tell your partner how you feel, and how you'd like more affection.

4. If they're a bit defensive on it, ask why.

5. If there is upset there, talk it out, so that you can have a better, more fulfilled relationship with one another.

This goes with all sorts of intimacy, whether it is in the bedroom, or even just physical intimacy before you have sex. You need to talk to your partner. Most therapists agree that we don't talk to our partners as much as we should, and that's what's hurting a lot of relationships. Talking to your partner and telling them how you feel is critical to a successful relationship, so remember that.

Touch More

This kind of ties into the point before, but if you notice that you're only touching in bed, it might be why you're not getting your needs fulfilled. You should realize that if you want to have sex, you need to let your partner know well before you even get into the bedroom.

Sometimes, you may need to send the signals out early on

before it does happen. Here are a few steps you can take, and a few things that you can do to help push affection, and get your needs met more.

1. Give a long kiss in the morning, maybe even have it get hot and heated, but then later on just leave it. That alone will increase the touch and keep it all alive.

2. Identify your love languages together and figure out what sorts of acts can help build intimacy, whether it is through touching one another, various acts that you two do together, giving various gifts, or spending time together. Just do that more, and hint at the fact that you want to spend more personal intimate time together.

3. Touch your partner more, a little lingering touch before they go to work can help get your partner's attention and get them going.

4. Don't be afraid to play a little hard to get, where you're affectionate, but then pull back. That alone can get them to come to you, begging for more.

For many people, this can be a hard practice to begin with, and for many, touching might be the one thing you're lacking in your relationship. But, by touching the one that you love more, you'll be much happier, and you'll be able to rev up the affection and intimacy with one another before you get between the sheets.

Don't Forget Foreplay

They always tell you to never skip foreplay, and that's true. Foreplay is one of the best ways to get sexual with your partner, and sometimes, people just skip that and go right to sex. This might seem like a good idea, but it doesn't enhance the experience, nor does it make it special for anyone.

So how do you do it? Well, there are a few ways to encourage foreplay with your partner, and if you're just having quickies everywhere, it's best if you try to create a good time to be sexual with one another.

Here are a few activities that you can use to help let your partner know that hey, you want to have sex, and you want to improve affection with one another:

• Schedule the time if needed

• Cuddle with your partner more

• Give sensual massages

• Read sexy poetry together

• Touch one another, and progress with intimacy

• Tell your partner through sexual language that you want them

When it comes to sex, foreplay is something that we always say never to skip. I'm sure that you've read that before, and oftentimes, people don't realize how important it is to never skip this. Foreplay is how the two of you basically communicate to one another that you want to have sex. It's one of the single most important aspects of sex that you need to remember, and if you aren't focusing at least on a little bit of foreplay, you're going to struggle.

Affection can be something you sometimes have to ask for straight up. Being forthright and honest might seem a little bit tacky and immature, but sometimes, the best way to communicate is by being honest, and not some beat-around-the-bush way.

It is embarrassing, I get that, but remember, this is the way for you two to communicate better, and in many instances, if your partner is looking to try and understand you better, communicating your physical intimacies is imperative. You should be honest about the way that you feel, and what you want.

We'll talk more about how you can ask for what you want in the bedroom in the next section.

Practice 24: Tell Me What You Want — Getting Your Needs Met in the Bedroom

Getting your needs met in the bedroom is super important because if you're not getting them met, you're going to be unhappy.

That's just the reality of it. If the needs aren't met, sex will seem like a chore. Maybe the two of you fell into bed perfectly, but you're feeling like you're missing something. Sometimes, you probably fell in love first before even explored what happened in the bedroom, and you notice there is a lot lacking here. Well, figuring out what you can do to get your needs met in the bedroom will help you figure out how to communicate with your partner.

One of the best ways to figure this out is by yourself, and know your body. One thing people tend to forget is that not everyone is the same. Not everyone will have an orgasm the same way, and some people will orgasm from things that they normally wouldn't orgasm from. Sometimes, exploring what makes your body feel good is just as important as sex.

Some of the ways you can do that include the following:

• Masturbate more and figure out where you like to be touched.

• Have your partner experiment with you and sometimes let them test a few things.

• Maybe tell them, if you're doing this, what you like, and where you like to be touched.

Yes, again this can be a bit awkward to discuss with your partner, but it's a wonderful means for you to let your partner know how you feel, and how you can be pleased through sex.

Connect Outside of the Bedroom

One way to ask for what you want is to literally, just ask, but that involves connecting outside of the bedroom. Have you ever tried to connect with a partner outside of the bedroom that you don't have any real connection with? It's awkward and oftentimes, that will mean you won't get your needs met.

You should understand that you need to be connected on another level, not just in the bedroom.

How to do this includes the following:

1. First, spend time with your partner outside of the bedroom.

2. Make sure that they're receptive outside of the bedroom.

3. Encourage doing nice things for them.

4. Set time aside to talk about this together.

5. Talk about how you want to try something new in the bedroom, or you want to get certain needs met.

This is important because, for real physical intimacy, you need emotional intimacy as well. Sex is great, it's a lovely thing to partake in with your partner, but if the two of you aren't telling the other person what you want, you're going to have a rough time together, both in and out of the bedroom.

Work on Encouragement

Encouraging your partner to continue doing something is the best way to handle sexual fulfillment in the bedroom. The problem with telling someone what you like at times is that people get in their feelings and feel like you're criticizing them. The best way to handle a change that you want in the bedroom is to be encouraging of what they're currently doing.

Why is that? It allows for the following to be communicated:

- That you're happy with the results

- That you want them to keep going

- That you want them to continue in that direction

- Allows for you to be more upfront immediately

Lots don't realize that being upfront with their partner currently will help them down the road, and in turn, will help to build better communication, so if you're upfront about this right now, you'll be more open to the different things you want to try later on, and it makes everyone much happier too.

Be Specific

It might seem strange but specifying what you want will help your partner know exactly what to do. Sometimes, saying "be rougher with me" is too vague. Where do you want to be rough? Do you want to be slapped across the face, or spanked? It communicates two very different points, and you may want to be spanked, but you don't want to be slapped across the face.

Being specific will allow your needs to be met.

How do you be specific though? Well, why not try the following:

- First, know what you want to change.

- Instead of using a question, use a statement, such as "I like it when you stroke my inner thigh slowly," or "I like it when you spank me hard."

- Have some emphasis behind the words you say, don't just laxly tell your partner that you like something.

- Encourage them to continue that with a statement, rather than a question.

This is one of the best ways to get what you want. That's because people respond better to direct instructions. Think about it, if you ask your partner to do something with a statement, then they'll do it. You state that you like it when they take care of cleaning up the house, then they'll respond better and clean the house.

On the flip side, if you're just saying "you could clean the house" they may say yes, but then not do it. It isn't much of a statement, just a suggestion. If you state what you want in the bedroom, being specific, then it will help.

Specifying what you want is incredibly important for you and your partner, and you need to make sure you're both on the same page in terms of what you both desire from sex and from life in general.

Practice 25: Their Needs Matter Too—What Your Partner Wants from Sex and How You Give It

Remember that it isn't just your show, it's your partner's show too. This is very good for a lot of people to learn, because oftentimes, if you only care about yourself, and not your partner, it will put you on a one-way train to disaster. Talking about what your partner wants out of this is very important, and you two should always talk this out together.

There are a few reasons why you need to talk to your partner about this, and they include the following:

- It fosters communication about needs between both of you, which is always good.

- It helps you perform better in a bedroom so you know what your partner likes.

- Sex isn't a one-person activity unless you're masturbating, so make sure that you're both on the same page for this.

- Working together on what both of you want is very important, so you can help create a better, more worthwhile relationship out of this together.

So how do you talk to your partner about what their needs are met? There are a few things the two of you can do together, and a couple of things that can ultimately benefit both of you. Here are a few ways to find out what your partner likes, and how to have this kind of conversation with them.

Have Them Show You

If you notice that you're not totally sure what they want in bed, have them show you. This can be sexy at times, and even just saying it in a lustful voice is a wonderful way to get them interested in you, and to get the heat going. This is a good way to encourage your partner to tell you explicitly what they desire because for many, having them show you what they want will prove more useful to both of you.

It can get embarrassing but telling your partner the truth about how they should do something that will benefit both of you in the long run. It can help build communication and trust as well.

What are some ways to practice this? Why not try the following:

• First, ask them what they want

• Have them show you what you want by asking nicely

• Have them be specific in what they want

• If they're embarrassed, tell them that you won't judge them for their needs

When it comes to building a relationship with your partner on a sexual level, talking about what turns you on can be a bit awkward for both of you, but it will help both of you when it comes to pleasuring and making the other person feel good. Plus, if you're going to be having sex with your partner, it's only right to make sure that they're just as happy with it as you are.

Consider Their Feelings

While it might seem a bit strange, considering the feelings of your spouse is just as important as ever. They're your spouse, and often, their feelings matter just as much as your own. You need to think before you speak, and you should always have the intent of learning about what your spouse likes before you start doing anything else.

To encourage your spouse to discuss this subject, you can always talk to them in a manner that allows them to speak freely.

Some tips for talking about this include the following:

• Don't sound like you're about to punish them

• Don't be accusatory, but instead curious

• Work on trying to understand, with that at the forefront of the communication

When talking to your partner about this subject, it can get awkward, but you should always think about how to approach this, and if you both are on the same page in terms of working it out, then it will make things better.

Simply Ask!

Sometimes, the solution to a dwindling sex life is to simply ask your partner about what's happening, and what's going on.

This is a good way to encourage your partner to talk. Asking them about what's happening, and whether or not they like something is incredibly important. That's because people don't realize what is going on, and what they need to do. If you notice that you're not talking in the bedroom, start to ask questions.

Ask them if they like it, where they would like to be touched, what makes them tick. Asking is the key to success, and it's one of the focal ways to improve your sex life. Sometimes, both of you are too embarrassed to ask about this, so don't be afraid to get the courage to ask and work things out together.

Asking in a way that's calm and collected, but also has the intent of improving the relationship will help both of you, and it's one of the best ways to figure out what they want. They will tell you, and it also does communicate to your partner that you care about them, and that they matter at the end of the day.

Make sure you're communicating your own interest and understand that it can make things easier.

Improve Your Mood

Sometimes, setting the mood and improving it is what you need to do in order to have better sex, and to ask them what they want. Sometimes, your home life might be chaotic, and that means that the mood isn't there for sex. If you have distractions that are in place, you should make sure that you take care of them beforehand. One way to communicate whether or not your partner is in the mood for sex is asking in a flirty manner about it, or maybe even set the mood by lighting candles, running a bath, and then getting into foreplay. If you notice that the mood is a little stagnated when having sex, then maybe change up what you're doing in the bedroom to help improve the general state of what's going on.

Some ways to improve the mood to help with sex include the following:

• Take a nice bath together

- Light some candles

- Burn some incense

- Kiss and touch your partner

- Cuddle together on the couch while watching a movie you both like

These are all simple little activities, but when it comes to actively improving your relationship, it does a whole lot of good.

The truth is, the reason why you're struggling with your relationship is that you don't have the mood set. The hustle and bustle of work, kids, and the like can take a toll on both of you.So make sure that you work on the mood as well as getting the courage to ask your partner as it will help foster that communication with one another.

Listen for the Sounds

The best way to know whether or not you're doing something correctly, is to listen for the signals and sounds. What that means is, listen for your partner's words, moans, or the like.

If you hear your partner making cute little moans when you touch them in certain places, then that's great, that's a wonderful way to get the responses you're looking for. Sure, you can explicitly ask if they like something, but sometimes, they may not even tell you.

The sounds your partner makes are just as important as what

you're doing. They help to communicate whether or not they like something, and also what you can do better. It can be a bit weird to listen for this, but if you do spend time listening and acknowledging these sounds, then you'll benefit from this. For a lot of people, learning your partner's sounds is a great way to understand your partner too, and in turn, it can help push you in the right direction.

For many couples, listening for this also builds mindfulness.

How you can listen to your partner's signals includes the following:

- Hearing them

- Asking them if they enjoy it

- Continue to hear any different moans or utterances of encouragement

- If you don't hear this, ask them if they like it in a sensual manner. They'll tell you honestly if not

By listening, you're building more understanding for them, and it can help to give your partner what they want. Remember, it takes two to tango, and sometimes, you might not even realize that your partner is unhappy with something sexually until they tell you. You might believe they like something when actually they can't stand it. We don't realize this until more often than not it's too late, and it can be a struggle, but it's worth trying and improving upon.

Practice 26: Proven Ways to Spice Up Your Sex Life and Have More Passion

So how can you improve your sex life? There are a few things you can do, and some activities that you can do to help you improve your sex life. Here, we'll highlight a few activities you can do yourself, and tips to help you have amazing sex.

Educate Yourself

The human body is interesting, and sex can be an ever-evolving activity. One of the best things you can do to help improve your sex life is a little bit of education.

Educating yourself doesn't mean you're stupid, it means that there is more to learn about the activity at hand. Learning about what makes your partner tick, and some of the things you can try with your partner lets you experiment in the bedroom.

Some ways you can learn about different sexual activities or different ways to pleasure your partner include the following:

• Books

• Various articles

• Any media on sex positions

While some may say porn, not all porn is educational in that regard. Remember, porn is a fantasy, and while those fantasies can come to life, they oftentimes aren't as easy to recreate as you think. Plus, lots of times they skip foreplay in porn, so why would you base everything off that? Porn can give you ideas, yes, but understand that it isn't the full answer to everything.

While many learn from experimenting, sometimes reading up on different ways to pleasure your partner can help you build a better understanding of what makes your partner tick. Learning is fun, and there is a lot to understand. Plus, sometimes learning and trying new things can be a fun adventure for both of you.

Try New Positions

Sometimes, just trying a new position can change your sex life. The Kamasutra exists for a reason, and people use this to learn new positions that they can try with their partner.

While a few of them are a bit too much for the average person, if there is a sex position that you've always wanted to try, then this is the time. Communicate with your partner that you want to try it, and from there, work it out together.

If you notice it isn't going to work, or it's not that comfy, then don't despair. Sometimes, those positions aren't always the way to go, but spicing things up through experimentation is a wonderful way to learn about your partner's body. Plus, it is a great bonding experience for both of you too, which is never a bad thing for couples that are going through a rut.

Use Lube

Seriously, use it. If you notice that it's a bit painful to have sex, you should consider adding lubricants and gels. Lots of people believe lube is just used for anal sex, but that isn't the case. Vaginal dryness occurs, and if you're older or going through premenopause, it can be a bit awkward and painful for you. If you want to make sex feel good for you, and your partner, have some lube on hand.

Lube can be put in a little soap dispenser on the bed, so it can take a couple of pumps to get it out. That saves the awkwardness of trying to fiddle around grabbing a bottle or spilling it all over the place.

For many people, they don't use lube, and the truth is, everyone's vagina is different. Some are drier than others, and some may not even realize they have an issue with vaginal dryness till it's too late so consider some lube as needed. Work on getting that in place in order to improve your sex life.

Write The Fantasies Down and Tell Your Partner

Everyone has fantasies or something that they want to do. If you notice that you have a fantasy that isn't communicated to your partner, it can stagger the relationship. Fantasies are something that should be fulfilled, within reason of course.

If you have fantasies that you know can be fulfilled by your partner, write these down. From there, communicate to your partner the fantasies that you have.

For example, if you've ever wanted to try a roleplay fantasy, communicate this to your partner. Tell them what you want, and sometimes, it can lead to sex just from discussing these fantasies alone. Hearing these from your partner can be a huge turn-on, and communicating the interests that you have deep down is incredibly healthy.

Lots of people don't realize how liberating it is to tell their partner about a desire that they have. And the best part is that it isn't a bad thing to have these either. People have their fetishes, their fantasies, but it's up to the other person to learn, understand, and acknowledge them. When they can't be acted out, sometimes even hearing about them can help improve your relationship and make things better. It can be wonderful fodder for bedroom fun.

So, if you have a fantasy that you've been itching to fulfill, write it down. It could change your sex life.

Use Toys

Toys are something people look down upon because they think toys are only used for sex, and nothing more. But toys are a wonderful addition to bedroom fun, and they are a great way for you to understand your body and improve on it.

Toys such as the following should be considered when looking to improve your relationship.

- Vibrators

- Dildos

- Cock rings

- Any stimulation toys

- Anything that might stimulate the senses

Sometimes, a toy is a wonderful addition to the bedroom. The reason why toys are looked down upon is that people think they will replace your partner. They don't, they're an addition to the bedroom that can help you learn and understand one another. Building a better, more worthwhile relationship involves learning to stimulate your partner, and sometimes, a toy helps with that.

Toys are wonderful because they can be used to help you improve your own understanding of your body, and the stimuli needed. It can teach you where you feel good, what makes you tick, and what you like. From there, you communicate it to your partner.

Plus, limiting your vision is a wonderful way to help you feel more. Did you know that if one sense is dulled, the others get heightened? This is no exception in the bedroom, so if you've been curious about whether or not it will affect things, the answer is yes it will. It can help with making you feel more, making you understand more, and it can change your sex life.

Why not give it a shot? Toys are fun and can be wonderful for couples to experiment.

Sexual Rendezvous

Sometimes, the way to improve your sex life is to roleplay, or even go on a getaway with just the two of you. Experimenting with this can help you improve your life.

The idea of roleplay is to help push away the stigma that you have to perform perfectly. Sometimes, an alternate persona or character will help you with improving your ability to perform.

Some couples like to take it so far as putting together a backstory, but even just dressing up and putting on a different person can help you improve your sex life.

Traveling is fun too, and it can help you with improving intimacy. It doesn't take much either. Some ways you can do it include going hiking or camping, visiting a new place in town, or even just going out to another city.

Couples who work together and try out new things together will realize that they have a spark there. Sexy trips are also a good way to get away from the mundane or boring. If you feel like your sex life has stagnated, you can improve on this by experimenting and building for some different activities for yourself that can benefit both of you.

Trips also don't have to be this super hammed up thing either. Instead, they can be fun little adventures you go on with the person that you love, and in turn, you two can build intimacy. Plus, spending time together will change the way you respond to sexual situations, and it can build that spark.

Sex is something lots of people don't focus on, because they believe you have to fix everything else first before you fix the sex life.

While yes, sex is secondary to the rest of it, the happy couples in life have it, and if you feel like your sex life is stagnating, then you need to do something about it. The right mindset and attitude will improve your ability to handle it all, and in turn, it will change your life. So, don't be afraid to work on improving it, making it better, and working on you.

BONUS CHAPTER: IMPROVE YOUR COMMUNICATION USING EMOTIONAL MANAGEMENT

Emotional Intelligence or EQ exists as the aptitude towards sensing and handling feelings. An advanced EQ helps people to interact well, reduce their stress and worry, defuse conflicts, perk up dealings, have concern for other people, and the gift of knocking out the trials that come with life. It is vital in interaction because feelings hold a big part in communication.

The skill of being aware of feelings or emotional awareness can help people succeed when relating to others. It helps in noting the feelings of others and how these feelings influence the manner they speak or communicate. EQ and emotional maturity are key aspects in keeping wholesome affairs, be it in marriage, friendship, or at the workplace.

Instead of blaming someone else for a problem or action, these emotionally mature people seek to revise the action or solve the problem. They hold themselves liable for their choices and actions without the need to lie in tough settings. Instead, they confront the truth head-on.

In any quarrel, they refrain from making any attack on the person and simply address the matter at hand. They are cautious in speaking and ensure their calmness by thinking before speaking. They respect limits and never depend on the childish defense process of rebound. If you are emotionally intelligent, then you can simply detect and control your own feelings.

You can sense emotions, besides proactively acting in response, instead of reactively. And because people with high EQ are in control of their feelings, they can put them well into words. They accept these feelings as they are and do not even try to disguise them by way of some other emotion. They use them as needed in terms of thinking or solving problems, mostly in dealings.

After all, when you have a dispute with someone, it is normal to feel a certain emotive response, which is adverse by and large. Hey, nothing is wrong with going through an adverse emotional response, but the way you use this response later makes all the honor or disgrace. Indeed, it requires some change in your mindset and can be quite hard to perfect.

Still, starting to tackle these settings in a mature, as well as wise manner, is where the wisdom sets off, and all else is a change for the better from there. Emotional management and maturity work together. You need your emotional management skills to recognize your feelings. Simultaneously, your emotional maturity will help you not to show your feelings reactively.

And this is essential in managing relationships. To properly find these qualities in a partner, you have to ensure that you possess those skills to start with. Why? Well, without those skills in you, you will not be capable of recognizing and acknowledging in others whatever you need yourself. So, work first on yourself, as this is the initial step in creating healthy and long-lasting relationships.

When you have accomplished this, help your spouse or partner work on his or her emotional maturity and intelligence. Remember that emotional maturity and intelligence requires constant, conscious training. Also, there may be instances when you will not perfect this skill. With diligence and dedication, though, you will eventually develop it and find it as a true indication of your growth. And when you can do this with your spouse or partner, that is what I meant when I said, "grow up together.

How to Work on Bettering Your Emotional Management

Some people possess an incredibly great IQ but minimal EQ, like a nutty scientist who cannot match his clothes. Other people possess incredibly high emotional intelligence but low general intelligence. And this can be seen in a street vendor, who cannot even write his name, yet can somehow convince you to buy his merchandise even when you may not personally need it.

Perhaps, this is among the reasons why psychologists sometimes assert that EQ is actually far important than IQ. The problem is that, unlike IQ, it is not stable and it's difficult to measure EQ. On top of that, it is mostly subjective. In contrast, EQ can be made better as compared to the stable IQ. So, you can develop it as you would work on your muscles or expertise and watch it grow.

Most of all, you do not need a high IQ to do this! Cool, right? The question now is how. Technically speaking, the skills drawn in EQ are awareness and regulation of one's self, motivation, empathy, besides social skills. And all these require patience, appreciation, gratitude, respect, and anger management. It would be best to first work on the last five qualities to facilitate the acquisition of the five first mentioned skills. So, let me present them to you in such an order.

Patience

This virtue assists in building empathy towards other people. If things do not go as you want them to, instead of entertaining that feeling of frustration, learn patience. Try seeing things and settings as a blessing in disguise or develop a positive mindset to have a happier life. When in an exasperating conversation, try listening well to the speaker and give yourself time to process your thoughts before saying anything.

A person needs enough patience to maintain harmony in his private, professional, and social life. And in relationships, patience is an essential element. By grasping the impact of patience, anyone can create peace in his relationships, which can transform his life for the better. You can be more patient in your relationship by first knowing your partner as an imperfect person like you are.

Next, accept the shortcomings of your partner or spouse. At the same time, let your spouse know you, as well, through regular communication. Make sure to listen to your partner when he is communicating verbally or nonverbally. Allow your spouse to be free to show you his real self and dedicate some time together, even in silence.

If your partner has the tendency to be grumpy, do not react in the same manner. For as long as you keep your communication lines open at all times, and you are determined to develop more patience, you will get by.

Appreciation, Gratitude, and Respect

Have you observed how the lack of appreciation looks like an increasing problem with all pairs, married or not, but have been living together for some years? If you believe that your partner has stopped appreciating your presence in this life, then you would agree with me when I say that appreciation is important in all healthy relationships!

As a human being, I believe that we constantly thirst for attention, which can only be done through appreciation. The problem begins when we fail to notice that we are slipping into the custom of taking our other half for granted. When this happens, we stop showing care and appreciation for our spouse. This causes other problems, like arguments, feelings of frustration, and resentment.

Then suddenly, probably after a big fight, we begin wondering if the relationship can be worked out or heading out of the door. Let us recall a common and simple scenario. Your spouse always brings your children to school and fetches them for home each and every school day. It has become a routine that you never showed any appreciation for.

Honestly, tell me. Are you not grateful that your partner is there to do this every school day since your children started going to school? Can you imagine its effect on your daily life if he simply stopped doing it for one day? Of course, you will need to make changes in your schedule for the day to accommodate this task. Probably, you will have to out of bed earlier than usual.

Would you be happy not watching your morning news show on TV because you also need to drop off the kids before going to work? Then, pick them up again from work in time after school? Yes, it is something simple, but can suddenly become important once not done! I remember asking a work colleague whose wife does this task if he ever thanked her for diligently doing it.

Guess his response! He frowned at me and replied, "What is there to thank her for that when they are understood to be done anyway?" I smiled and slowly walked away, knowing that my work colleague thinks that he is doing bigger things than what his spouse does. And that is where the stability in relationships begins to go off the scale. Appreciation remains vital to any relationship.

Valuing someone can make them feel happy about whatever they are doing. And that can make a difference in their existence. They feel better about themselves, urging them to keep on with fresh vigor, and strengthening their relationship. Interested in knowing if your spouse lacks appreciation? It is actually easy as certain signs imply being undervalued in a relationship, as follows:

1. There are now arguments over trivial things;

2. Lately, your spouse starts getting more emotional;

3. Perhaps, they talk less now as compared to before;

4. Opinions are no longer asked;

5. Plans are made without consulting the other;

6. Less enthusiastic about occasions, such as anniversaries and birthday;

7. Poor sex life; and,

8. Preference for more time away from each other.

Appreciation has two aspects, specifically one based on focus and the other on time. Time-based appreciation exists slightly like a puzzle as you either turn out to be angrier with the behavior of your partner or become more patient. Now, which turns out is an issue of outlook. Acceptance begins from your awareness that things remain not likely towards changing over time, hence, you turn out more accepting.

When this happens, it is easier for you to appreciate what he/she does. If you alter your viewpoint, you may get even used to their most irritating ways and find some importance in them. Besides, this lets you focus on whatever makes them happy. So, in what way can you display your appreciation towards your partner? At hand are certain things you can try, as follows:

1. Admit what you are fond of about your spouse, his family, and friends;

2. Appreciate all that adds importance to your bond and regularly tell your spouse about it;

3. Compliment him on simple matters, such as saying "I love the way that printed tie enhances your professional look!"

4. Enjoy your moments together by being lively while appreciating one another;

5. Focus fully on whatever your partner is saying and make eye contact to assure him that you value whatever he is telling you;

6. Thank him for little stuff, such as ironing your clothes, doing the laundry, or cooking food when you feel too tired or lazy to do them. Examples are the following lines:

a. "I am really grateful for your washing up the dishes after supper."

b. "Honey, I love the way you help me prepare my things each morning while I dress up for the office. It makes me feel so special!"

c. "Thank you so much for coming into my life, dear. I wonder how I can go through life without you by my side!"

7. Most importantly, regularly express your gratitude and affection for your spouse.

Healthy relationships stand those that keep growing and, in terms of love, appreciating your partner is never sufficient. When you invest so much in relations, it feels delightful to receive an acknowledgment for the effort. So, make appreciating your spouse a priority towards keeping the spark perky.

Anger Management

When you create a romantic bond, you carry this out with your unique personalities formed by your previous relationships. So, each has developed notions about the way the beloved should react to your desires, needs, and expectations. Additionally, you have well-established patterns that include the manner you manage annoyance when your loved one appears to ignore your desires, needs, and expectations.

It is then unsurprising that, irrespective of how loving your relationship is, at times anger and conflict happens. And this is particularly challenging when both or one of you are prone to irritation. While having conflicts now and then is usual for couples, once they become intense and frequent, they can negatively impact the physical, mental, and family well-being of a household.

The prospective for such effect especially arises once both or one of the partners is susceptible to anger. And destructive anger within relationships can cause sadness, increased dissatisfaction, and thoughts of abuse, isolation, and eventually divorce. Irrespective of the way you studied on dealing with disagreements, it is essential to bear in mind that there are specific flairs that support positive management of conflict, including recovering from conflicts.

Always bring to mind that the nastiest time to quarrel is when you are furiously angry because it is when you are more prone to concentrate on your personal grievances and not ready to listen to your partner. So, allow me to share with you a clear set of tactics to deal with conflict that is rooted in self-awareness, mindfulness, and empathy for your partner and yourself. I urge you to share these strategies with your spouse and have a signed pledge to observe them as we did.

1. Commit to practicing healthy anger as the foundation for constructively dealing with conflicts in your relationship. So, when your partner remains quick to anger, it is best not to respond in anger as well, and instead listen to him. If you are the one who is quick to anger, take time outs.

2. Only when both of you have controlled your anger can you carry out a proper sharing in a concession and solve your problem. This means that each should focus on specific actions, not on statements uttered by an angry partner. More-

over, when both are sufficiently relaxed, then it is time for you to discuss your differences.

3. Both should agree to stop the discussion and have a time-out when any partner feels too worked up or intensely uncomfortable. Additionally, set limits regarding using bad language, yelling, behaving in an abusive manner, or threatening. In our case, we agreed to use the word "Time-out" to signal the need to cease further argument for a while.

4. Ideally, it is best to resume whatever activity is ongoing or planned before the conflict. In certain cases, though, solitude is needed. When this happens, the person wanting some time alone just utters our agreed phrase of "Tea Break."

Generally, we just comfortably proceed with our activity together without talking about the disagreement until we are both calm. When the magic words "Tea Break" are spoken though, the speaker will have our bedroom all for himself until he comes out or calls out for the other to come in. We have agreed on this instead of leaving home to prevent triggering the other to feel further anxiety, especially when sensitive to the issue abandoned.

5. When we decide towards stopping a discussion with no resolution, we generally resume the talk when both are sufficiently relaxed. This is because we have made a commitment to solving issues. And if the feeling of anger escalates on the next discussion, we stop to calm down, as well as trying again a few days later.

6. If our argument concerns important issues, unsettled conflicts will pop up again. So, failing to talk about identified issues only damages this entire arrangement. Nevertheless, we also have to be aware of time limitations since both of us are working.

7. Thus, our agreed discussion period is a maximum of an hour. If unresolved, then it is resumed later in the same day, the day after, or any other agreed day when both have no other commitments and are calm. We also set rules on conducting discussions, such as never in front of the children or in our bedroom.

8. And when issues are fully addressed, we individually apologize for our respective share to the conflict and tension. In this way, we reaffirm our respect, trust, and love for each other.

These guidelines have made my marriage stand the test of time. I am sharing this with you with the prayer that it will help you somehow bridge any communication gap you may have with your partner. Having differences is expected once you go into a deep relationship. And once they take place, your challenge is to communicate constructively.

Managing conflict through this manner remains a crucial ingredient aimed at a more pleasing relationship. So, take time to appease yourself enough towards thinking about whatever you are annoyed about. Remember that your annoyance is revealing something about your personality. Although the anger is frequently aimed at your spouse, it is always more concerning you than concerning your spouse.

Awareness

Without this trait, trying to handle your emotions is like sitting inside a tiny dinghy without direction atop the ocean of your personal emotions totally at the fancy of the tides of whatever exists happening each moment. Having no idea of where you are going, all you could do is yell for assistance.

Awareness of one's self involves understanding your actions on three stages, specifically, what you are doing; the way you feel regarding it; and the hardest of them all, figuring out whatever you do not see about yourself. In the first stage, we tend to do things nowadays on autopilot.

For example, wake up each day to wash your face, brush your teeth, prepare breakfast, wake up the kids and hubby, feed the pets, take the kids to school, go to the gym, market, or home, and so on. To develop self-awareness, you can try scheduling time or a day to break the monotony. For example, setting 10 minutes in the day to just think of your life and how you are feeling.

Once you really focus on your feelings, which is the second stage, it can be scary in the beginning. You might realize how often you are actually pretty depressed or go through a great deal of anxiety. At this moment, it is important not to judge the feelings that arise as it can just make things worse.

Instead, have faith that whatever emotion stays there holds a good purpose for being there even when you cannot remember that reason. Once you spot all the uncomfortable stuff you are feeling, you will begin to sense where your personal vulnerable points are.

For instance, when I am speaking and someone interrupts me, I really get irritated. Upon being aware of these points, I can start figuring out how do deal with my emotions and do something about them, which is the final stage.

Regulation of One's Self

This requires the ability to channel your feelings well. People who are certain that emotions exist as life's be-all-end-all often seek habits to regulate their emotions. Truth is, you cannot, as you can just respond to them. Feelings are purely the signs that prompt us to focus on something. Then, it is our choice to consider whether "something" is important or not, besides finding the best action to address it or ignore it.

What I would like to stress here is the fact that there is no "bad" or "good" emotion, but only "bad" or "good" responses to emotions. For example, anger is a destructive feeling when misdirect and hurt yourself or others in the course of action. In contrast, it is a good feeling when used to protect others or yourself. Similarly, joy is a wonderful feeling when imparted to people you hold dear when something great happens.

It is a horrifying feeling, however, when it is derived from harming others. Such as the action of handling your emotions, which is recognizing what you are feeling, deciding if that is an appropriate feeling for the circumstances, and acting given that.

Motivation

Have you learned to inspire yourself? When you are motivated to do something, you can lose yourself wholly in it. The best example for this is when you start on something, get engrossed in it that, when you suddenly look at the clock, you realize you have been doing it for four hours but felt like 20 minutes! This happened often during the writing of this book.

Honestly, I adore this emotion, and once I pull it off, it inspires me to go on writing. Take note that I do not expect that emotion to arise in advance of my starting to write. I begin writing, and when that feeling commences building towards motivating me to write more, the feeling encourages me more. Thus, when you take action, it is not merely the result of inspiration, but likewise its cause.

Alas, most people look for motivation first for them to take some important action and modify themselves, besides their situation. These people try to fill themselves up using whatever zest of mental stimulation is trendy that week for them to finally make a start. By the next week, however, they have depleted their steam and back at the starting line in search of another motivation method.

My point here is that to use your feelings effectively to take action, you simply have to start something. Pay attention to your feelings before, during, as well as after all that you are doing and utilize those emotions as a guide to your future actions. And I am not just talking here about "good" feelings because sometimes frustration and annoyance can also motivate people to take action.

Empathy

Would you agree with me when I say that recognizing the emotions of other people can create healthier relationships? Have you observed that everything we have covered at this point deals with managing and directing feelings within yourself? The whole idea of improving emotional management, however, is to foster healthier bonds in life.

These healthy relationships begin with recognizing and respecting the emotional needs of others. You carry this out by bonding with and having compassion for others. Through listening to other people and honestly sharing yourself with them is actually being vulnerable to them. After all, to relate to someone does not necessarily require your understanding them completely.

Instead, the requirement is for you to accept this person as he or she is, even without fully understanding them. What is essential here is your learning to cherish their existence, besides treating them not as a means aimed at something else. In this way, you get to acknowledge their discomfort as your discomfort and as a collective discomfort. Relationships are anywhere the emotional rubber strikes the proverbial roadway. They get people out of their heads and enter the world surrounding them. They make people realize we are a slice of something far larger and more complex than only ourselves.

Ultimately, relationships remain the manner we express our values. So, we must infuse our emotions with standards. Otherwise, emotional management is meaningless, lacking orientation of your morals. For example, a father may teach his kid the creeds of emotional management. Without also educating him on the tenets of respect and honesty, his kid can become emotionally intelligent and a ruthless liar!

In the end, we are always choosing whatever we value consciously and unconsciously. And our feelings will execute those values in motivating our actions in certain ways. So, to properly have the life truly wanted, you need to initially be clear on what you truthfully value because that is where the energy of your emotions will be heading for. And knowing whatever you truly cherish, not just whatever you declare you cherish, is perhaps the utmost emotionally intelligent ability you can improve.

How to Communicate Through Difficult Emotions

Thoughts and feelings are different, however, they are related to one other like a coin's tail and head. Though we are not fully conscious of them, our reaction to events is our primary emotion, through which general decisions are made. Feelings are sensations that are unlike thoughts, beliefs, understandings, and convictions. Once difficult feelings that exist are expressed, the pointed edges are blunted to make it easier to free the bad emotions.

If we just express our opinions about an event, not our feelings, the unhealthy feelings linger, besides they are often difficult to release. So, when someone speaks, "I sense that…," the individual is really about to state an opinion, not his feeling. At this point, allow me to share the guidelines we use at home when expressing feelings.

1. Commitment to be exact, rather than vague, about how we feel.

Consistently using just a word or two to say the way one feels, like bad or distressed, is too general. So, be specific, such as anxious, irritated, sad, hurt, afraid, sad, or lonely.

Also, stating the extent of the emotions will bring down the odds of being misjudged. For example, several people may interpret, "I am mad," as meaning extremely irate when you in fact just mean a little annoyed.

2. When expressing irritation, first describe the specific action you dislike, then your sentiments.

This helps in preventing other people from becoming instantly defensive or frightened when they hear you say that you are angry with them. If you experience mixed feelings, then say so, as well as explaining your ambivalence.

An example is saying, "I have varied feelings about your behavior. I am happy and grateful that you assisted me, but I do not like your comment about me being stupid. I find it disrespectful, unnecessary, and irritating." In the process, my partner and I discovered that using "I" messages help us to express our feelings productively.

3. We have agreed to respectfully confront each other when one is bothered by the behavior of the other.

This entails allowing each other to express difficult sensations without offending the pride of the other. And to do this, each should clarify, first to himself/herself and then to the other, precisely what is felt. In this manner, we can prevent emotions from piling up and grow into contempt and resentment.

4. We understand that we need to communicate difficult emotions in a way that lessens the need for the other to become self-protective and boosts the chances that the other will listen.

Practical Exercises to Try with Your Partner to Improve Communication

1. Think concerning your response whenever you are sad and angry. Then, pay attention to what may be triggering that response. Did your partner say something true or incorrect? Did you feel they were attacking you as a person?

Next, ask your partner to go through the same exercise and share your individual responses without passing judgment on each other. In this way, you get an inner glimpse of the personality of your partner while allowing him or her the chance to know you better.

2. Try to remember a particular time wherein you were grumbling. Then, explain to yourself why you were upset and what you really felt. Were you able to tell your partner directly what you felt? If not, what made it so hard for you to say it?

3. What have your parents taught you on communication? Recall what they did when they were upset. Are you doing the same things? When you were still a child, in what way were you permitted to express your upset and angry moods? Is it still the same now that you have your own family?

CONCLUSION

Relationships are important. They are a connection with the person you care about, the one you love. If you notice it's stagnating, you need to do something about it.

This book showed you what you can do to improve your relationship with your partner. Remember, it doesn't have to be something major or drastic, but these little activities can take less than half an hour each day, and they foster habits within you that are incredibly important to your relationship.

So, what you need to take away from this book includes the following:

- Work on mindfulness with your partner
- Work on understanding your partner
- Build intimacy on an emotional level
- Work on your sex life

These 25 practices will help you understand your relationship better, and for many couples, there's a lot that you can do here to better it. It is incredibly important that you learn to better your relationship.

The one thing that I want you to take away from this, is that it's possible to rebuild a relationship. Even if you believe it's a sinking ship, you should work on building it, unless of course, the person is abusive and unhealthy for your life. If you know this person is good for you, is the one you love, and they make you happy, but there are relationship points that need to be fixed, then you should take the practices here, and work on them right away.

If you were happy once, you can be happy once again. Most don't believe that, and they offer a pessimistic view on life. But, if you know that you love the person you're with, and you know that it can be fixed, then you should do something about it. A doingness and fixing your relationship aren't done just through hoping it gets fixed. What you need to do is work on it, and work on improving your relationship. Your partner will be happy, and you'll be happy.

Relationships can be fixed, and by improving the emotional intimacy, physical intimacy, and mindfulness, you can make it possible.

RESOURCES

11 ways to help yourself to a better sex life. *Harvard Health.* **https://www.health.harvard.edu/healthbeat/11-ways-to-help-yourself-to-a-better-sex-life**

(4 Jul 2019) Emotional Intelligence in Relationships (+activities for couples) *positivepsychology.com.* retrieved from: **https://positivepsychology.com/emotional-intelligence-relationships/**

(3 May 2014). Relationship Rx: 9 Tips for Establishing Emotional. *HuffPost. Retrieved from:* https://www.huffpost.com/entry/relationship-rx-9-tips-fo_b_4890602

Building emotional intelligence for better relationships. *Psychology Today.* Retrieved from: https://www.psychologytoday.com/us/blog/conscious-communication/201806/building-emotional-intelligence-better-relationships

(07 May 2019) Hot to Tell your Partner What you want in Bed, because you deserve to enjoy yourself, too. *Elite Daily.* Retrieved from: **https://www.elitedaily.com/dating/sex/how-to-tell-your-partner-what-you-want-in-bed/2022685**

Building Emotional Intelligence for better relationships. *Psychology Today.* Retrieved from: https://www.psychologytoday.com/us/blog/conscious-communication/201806/building-emotional-intelligence-better-relationships

Five Ways Mindfulness Makes Your Relationship happier. *Psychology Today.* Retrieved from: https://www.psychologytoday.com/us/blog/the-mindful-self-express/201706/five-ways-mindfulness-makes-your-relationship-happier

(14 October 2015). 12 Reasons why Relationships Fail You Must know. *EnkiRelations.* Retrieved from: **https://www.enkirelations.com/why-relationships-fail.html**

(16 Oct 2016) How to Improve your Relationships with Mindfulness. *HuffPost.* Retrieved from: **https://www.huffpost.com/entry/how-to-improve-your-relat_b_8306260**

Printed in Great Britain
by Amazon